Spanish Golden Age Poetry

European Masterpieces
Cervantes & Co. Spanish Classics Nº 29

General Editor: TOM LATHROP
                    University of Delaware

Anthology of Spanish Golden Age Poetry

Edited and with notes by

R. JOHN MCCAW
University of Wisconsin—Milwaukee

and

KATHLEEN THORNTON SPINNENWEBER
Franciscan University of Steubenville

Cervantes & Co.

FIRST EDITION

Copyright © 2007 by European Masterpieces
270 Indian Road
Newark, Delaware 19711
(302) 453-8695
Fax: (302) 453-8601

MANUFACTURED IN THE UNITED STATES OF AMERICA

ISBN 978-1-58977-048-5

Table of Contents

Introduction to Students

POETRY PLAYED A VERY important cultural role in Spain throughout the sixteenth and seventeenth centuries—that is, the years 1500-1700, also commonly referred to as Spain's "Golden Age." And as Spain itself became a global power during these two centuries, the Spanish language and culture became established all over the world, and particularly in the Americas. Spanish poetry, in effect, followed suit. Intimately connected to song and music, poetry flourished at all levels of Spanish society as a medium of entertainment and instruction, as well as a source of imaginative thinking, religious affirmation, news, historical memory, and community bonding. For illiterate Spanish speakers, highly musical poems such as ballads (*romances*) and hymns were easy to remember, and formed part of the oral tradition. For educated and literate Spanish speakers, this oral tradition was very important, but also important was the literary tradition of written Spanish poems such as sonnets and *décimas*. Though nearly all of the poems in this anthology are polished works from the Spanish literary tradition, several became popular within the oral tradition.

All of the poems featured in this collection are masterpieces of Spanish Golden Age literature, but it must be noted that, for the sake of brevity, not all of the poetic masterpieces from the Golden Age have been included, and not all of the period's worthy poets are represented. The goal of this anthology, then, is not to provide an exhaustive survey of Spanish Golden Age poetry. The goal, rather, is to introduce students to several short and medium-length poems, and to help students improve vocabulary, grammar, cultural knowledge, reading strategies, and listening skills while studying these poems.

CULTURAL NOTES

This introduction cannot possibly discuss all of the cultural concepts and facts that may help facilitate understanding of the poems in this collection. However, even though we try to address specific cultural concepts and facts in the footnotes to individual poems, it may help you to know or review a few things in advance. There are many cultural dimensions to the poems in this volume, but some of the essential and recurring features of context and theme include religious beliefs and institutions, social structure and values, mainstream world views, and major literary trends and practices.

Catholicism and Church Culture

Many forces helped to shape Spanish culture during the sixteenth and seventeenth centuries, but the Church—that is, the Catholic Church—led the way in directing, regulating, and producing cultural activity such as literature, art, music, architecture, and scientific inquiry. The Church was the only officially approved religious institution in Spain, and it fought to combat non-Christian religious influences (chiefly, Judaism and Islam) as well as Christian movements considered heretical at the time (such as Lutheranism). Though the Catholic Church experienced many changes during the two centuries of Spain's Golden Age, and though various movements and trends of cultural interest emerged from the Church in Spain at the time, church officials placed a great deal of value on religious orthodoxy. Hence, the Spanish Inquisition, begun in the late fifteenth century for the purpose of monitoring the activities of Jews, became a major tool in the Church's quest to minimize dissent and promote official Church beliefs and practices.

The Catholic Church in Spain operated as part of the larger, far-reaching Roman Catholic Church headquartered in Rome, Italy. At the top of this organization were—and still are—the Pope, the Cardinals, and other high-ranking Church officials. In Spain, as in other countries, the Archbishops, then the Bishops, and then other officials exercised power and authority in the name of the Pope. Many poets in Spain held church offices, mostly at the local level. And just as Christianity, in the form of Catholicism, permeated all aspects of the lives of the Spanish people, it permeated much of the poetry of the age.

Mysticism

One of the most distinctive manifestations of Catholicism and Church culture in Spanish Golden Age poetry is mysticism, a person's highly intimate and often allegorical quest for spiritual union with God. Though religious mysticism in Spain has not been limited to Christianity (there are rich mystical traditions in Jewish and Muslim culture on the peninsula), and though Christian mysticism in Spain has often been influenced by Jewish and Muslim sources, mysticism in Spanish Golden Age poetry is decidedly a Catholic phenomenon. The most intense and well known expression of mysticism during this period took place in the latter half of the sixteenth century, exemplified by the poetry of Fray Luis de León, San Juan de la Cruz, and Santa Teresa de Ávila. The rise and development of mysticism during the Golden Age is strongly linked to the effects of the Catholic Church's reaction to the Protestant Reformation. As the theological beliefs espoused by Martin Luther, John Calvin, and others gained popularity in parts of Europe, the Catholic Church responded with its own program of renewal, now known as the Counter-Reformation. This initiative not only resulted in mysticism and mystic poetry, but also spawned other Catholic movements and activities including the founding of new religious orders (such as the Jesuits) and the reform of others (such as the Carmelites).

Monarchy, Aristocracy, and Court Culture

Alongside the Catholic Church in Spain existed another major institution with significant cultural impact: the Court. If the Church may be considered the main cultural vehicle in Spain for expressing and transmitting Christian ideas and practices, the Court in Spain may be understood as the primary cultural domain of society's most socially ambitious and politically privileged people. The King, representing the monarchy, stood at the apex of the Court hierarchy. Next in position were the grandees, the titled nobility of the aristocracy: the Dukes and Duchesses, the Marquises and Marquesses, and the Counts and Countesses. At the bottom of the hierarchy were the *hidalgos*, noblemen of the lesser aristocracy. They were also known as *caballeros*, and generally enjoyed the privilege of using the title *Don* before their name. Nobles at all levels were customarily employed to assist the King in a variety of roles ranging from political advisors to personal stewards.

Just as Church culture radiated from Rome throughout Spain and many other parts of the world by way of a far-flung network of cathedrals, churches, schools, palaces, and other spaces, Spanish Court culture—intimately and complexly connected with European court culture in general—spread from the royal residence (the court or capital) and throughout the rest of Spain. During the Spanish Golden Age, the towns of Toledo, Valladolid, and Madrid each served, at different times, as the court headquarters. But court culture also included a vast network of palaces, country estates, hunting grounds, diplomatic outposts, and other spaces throughout the Peninsula, the colonies, and beyond.

Court culture was essentially aristocratic culture. When male aristocrats were not busy working and networking at court, they spent time on leisure activities such as hunting, horseback riding, parlor games, reading, and writing. Aristocrats frequently participated in military activity on behalf of the King, and enjoyed martial activities such as fencing and jousting. Aristocratic women engaged in more domestic pursuits such as games, reading, writing, sewing, and conversation. A popular book on court culture, *Il Cortegiano* (1528) by Baldassare Castiglione, was translated into Spanish and published in 1534. This book, known in English as *The Book of the Courtier*, not only presents many details of aristocratic life, but also served as a how-to guide for aristocrats interested in becoming exemplars of court culture. The poets Juan Boscán (the translator of the Spanish version mentioned) and Garcilaso de la Vega (author of an introduction to Boscán's translation) both were considered prototypical examples of the poet-soldier Renaissance man of court culture.

Though Church and Court existed in Spain as separate institutions, they overlapped to a great extent: most high-ranking Church officials came from the aristocracy, and Catholicism was the religion of Spanish aristocrats. Indeed, Church culture was a kind of Court culture, and Court culture was an adjunct of Church culture.

Old Christians, New Christians, and Purity of Blood

In early Spain, a *cristiano viejo* was a Spaniard of pure Christian lineage, and that generally meant a descendant of the ancestral Roman-Gothic-Celtiberian race that populated much of the peninsula at the time of the Muslim invasion in 711. Technically, to be recognized as a *cristiano viejo*, one had to demonstrate ancestral purity and show oneself free from Jewish and Moorish lineage. In the Spanish Golden Age, it was generally thought a distinction to be considered of pure Christian heritage, in contrast to the *cristianos nuevos*, who were *conversos* (that is, Jews and Moors recently converted to Christianity). By the middle of the sixteenth century, statutes of *limpieza de sangre* ("purity of blood") became established and effectively limited access to political and ecclesiastical office on the basis of pedigree. Caste consciousness linked to *limpieza de sangre* cut across class lines, as aristocrats and commoners alike endeavored to prove, and sometimes purchase, *cristiano viejo* standing. In the popular imagination of the time, *limpieza de sangre* was primarily a concern of the grandees and *hidalgos*.

Honor

In sixteenth- and seventeenth-century Spain, many people—primarily from the aristocracy and middle class—made personal and professional decisions in accordance with concerns regarding reputation and public image. This concern for honor (*el honor*) and its counterpart, shame (*la vergüenza*), determined many a person's perceived worth and quality of life as evaluated by other people. This culture of honor in Golden Age Spain emerged from codes of behavior that derived from aristocratic courtly culture of the Middle Ages.

Cultural World View

The poems in this collection express other features of the world view held by many Spaniards of the Golden Age. One recurring feature is a sensitivity to change and the passage of time (*mudanza*), including a deeply felt understanding of the brevity of life, the fragility of humanity, and the inevitability of death. Though this outlook is often seen as pessimistic, it is also frequently represented in positive terms. Life was, of course, celebrated and cherished, but it was also generally seen as a mere prelude to an afterlife. Much of this ethos derives from the biblical teachings and popular beliefs promoted by the Catholic Church. But also important in forming this world view was the immediate, day-to-day experience of people who lived in an extremely polarized society. Most of the people in Spain dealt with disease, war, social immobility, and economic hardship at levels unimaginable to most residents of the Western world today. And even though the most privileged people—including many, but not all, aristocrats and artisans—enjoyed a far better quality of life and range of opportunities than the rest of Spanish society, they also faced steady challenges such as illness, social strife, political upheavals, and economic shifts.

People responded to life's vagaries and hardships in many different ways, but the poems in this collection show at least two distinctive trends. On the one hand, some people led lives of purposeful self-deprivation, frequently as a way to atone for their sins, manifest the suffering of humanity, and prepare for a better afterlife. Many different levels of self-deprivation existed, ranging from corporeal self-mortification (such as the wearing of hair shirts and the use of other objects that cause discomfort or pain) to the renunciation of worldly pursuits (such as gambling, drinking, or reading books). Regardless of the degree of self-deprivation, a main objective was to perceive the fleetingness of life and the transience of material objects, and to understand and transcend the trappings of human existence. In effect, the material, human world was seen as full of snares and deceptions (*engaños*) that obscured the more meaningful and enduring truths or revelations (*desengaños*) available to humanity. On the other hand, some people led lives of indulgence, often as a way to enjoy earthly pleasures that might be lost forever with old age and death. The injunction to "seize the day" (in Latin, *carpe diem*) also showed an interest in transcending the snares of the world, with the goal of experiencing epiphanies such as æsthetic beauty and sexual union.

Renaissance Cosmology and the Music of the Spheres

Throughout the Renaissance, including the Spanish Golden Age, people believed that the earth lay at the center of all creation, and that the rest of the known heavenly bodies were organized around the earth into concentric, revolving, celestial spheres. This belief, part of an earth-centered way of seeing the universe (that is, a geocentric cosmology), predominated since Antiquity, tracing its origins to the writing of Ptolemy, Aristotle, and other ancient thinkers. Even though various scientific discoveries in the Renaissance (by figures such as Copernicus, Newton, Kepler, Galileo) eventually led people in later centuries to abandon the geocentric model for a sun-centered (heliocentric) understanding, most people held onto the idea that several layers of spheres surrounded the earth. The spheres carried the known planets (including the moon, which was considered a planet) and the stars, and ended with the prime mover (*primum mobile*) at the outermost sphere. The spheres were thought to have mathematically proportional relationships to each other, and it was believed that instrumental music (characterized by intervals and harmony) was a manifestation of this proportionality. Lying beyond the spheres was the fixed, unmoving realm of God, known as the Empyrean. Some of the poems in this anthology, particularly those by Fray Luis de León, will refer to concepts related to the music of the spheres. Specific concepts and references will be explained in footnotes.

Petrarchism, Conceptismo, and Culteranismo

In fourteenth-century Italy, Francesco Petrarca emerged as a literary innovator whose impact has been felt in Spain since the fifteenth century. In his *Canzioniere* Petrarch—as he is known in the English-speaking world—established the genre of poems known as *sonnets*. In addition, Petrarch cultivated a distinctive style of poetic writing characterized by the playful opposition of words (antithesis) and by a polished, elegant rhetoric. Furthermore, Petrarch's poems revised some popular, centuries-old themes; chief among them was *courtly love*. Though other innovative poets in Petrarch's Italy cultivated sonnets and other poetic genres, experimented with poetic technique and rhetoric, and engaged with courtly love and other themes, Petrarch's work gained immense popularity throughout Europe and became the prototype for literary innovation in Spain and elsewhere. The poetry of the Spanish poets Juan Boscán and Garcilaso de la Vega, some of which begins this anthology, reflects Petrarchism's strong influence in Spain.

In addition to Petrarch, several other Italian writers—including Dante and Bembo—cultivated a poetic style that became very popular in Spain. This style, with Petrarchism at its center, was referred to as "la poesía italianizante," that is, Italianate Poetry. Still, as the poem by Cristóbal Castillejo indicates, not all poets embraced the "nuevo lenguaje" of the Italian poets. Castile and other regions of Spain had developed native forms of poetry throughout the Middle Ages, and many poets—such as Castillejo—saw Italianate Poetry as a strange and unwelcome development in Spanish culture.

Though earlier forms and styles of Spanish poetry persisted throughout the Golden Age, Italianate Poetry—and specifically, Garcilaso's version of Petrarchism—became the standard for poetic writing in Spain. Significantly, the works of Fray Luis de León, San Juan de la Cruz, and Santa Teresa show that Petrarchism even influenced religious poetry by the middle of the sixteenth century. In the late sixteenth century, after Italianate Poetry in Spain developed and matured over dozens of years, a related yet distinctive poetic style—later referred to as *conceptismo*—emerged. *Conceptista* poetry typically employs simple words and direct rhetoric in order to showcase clever metaphors, witty puns, and other conceptual forms of light wordplay. Francisco de Quevedo is often considered the most representative practitioner of *conceptismo*, though many other major poets—including Lope de Vega and Luis de Góngora—cultivated the style for at least a part of their literary career.

In the seventeenth century, another poetic style—later referred to as *culteranismo*—emerged and developed in stark contrast to *conceptismo*. *Culteranista* poetry characteristically mixes common Castilian words with erudite, Latin-style vocabulary in complicated, even convoluted, verses. As with *conceptista* poetry, clever metaphors, witty puns, and other forms of wordplay characterize *culteranismo*, but tend to be more densely embedded and more difficult to understand. Many readers from the seventeenth century to the present day have maintained that *culteranista* poetry places style over substance, and communicates little or no meaning. However, other readers have maintained that *culteranista* poetry—at least, the *culteranista* poetry cultivated by the most able poets—reveals a great deal of meaning. Luis de Góngora is generally considered the foremost *culteranista* poet, though not all of his poetry reflects the *culteranista* style. Góngora, whose signature style of *culteranismo* is referred to as *gongorismo*, feuded with several *conceptista* poets and theorists, including Quevedo and (to a lesser extent) Lope de Vega. Interestingly, Quevedo and Lope de Vega tried their hand at *culteranista* poetry—principally, but not exclusively, in order to poke fun at Góngora—with notable success. Many other important poets, such as Pedro Calderón de la Barca and Sor Juana Inés de la Cruz, successfully experimented with *culteranismo* in general and *gongorismo* in particular.

Classical, Biblical, and Other References
For centuries, Spanish poets have been making reference in their work to all sorts of figures and events associated with ancient texts. These texts were generally either biblical (i.e., the Old and New Testaments) or classical (i.e., mythology, history, and literature from Rome and Greece) in nature. A few writers also referred to texts from other ancient traditions, including religious works from Judaism and Islam, and fables and legends from Middle Eastern and Far Eastern cultures. In the Spanish Golden Age, poets from both Church and Court avidly incorporated classical, biblical, and other ancient references into their

work in order to emphasize points, create visual images, allude to subtle ideas, and demonstrate erudition. Generally speaking, the cultural trend in Golden Age Spain from which this impulse arose is known as Humanism. As the poems in this anthology show, some references—for example, the crucifixion of Christ, the imperial might of ancient Rome, and the Labyrinth of Dædalus—arise with great frequency, as they held a special place in the imagination of Golden Age poets.

As you read the poems, you will notice that not all references relate to ancient texts. Many Golden Age poets were interested in making reference to more recent texts, such as works in Italian by Petrarch and Dante. In addition, Golden Age poets routinely borrowed from and referred to literary works and oral texts from the Spanish tradition. With each new generation of poets in Golden Age Spain, there was more material in Spanish to draw from. For example, echoes of Garcilaso de la Vega's poetry are evident in the work of many subsequent poets. In effect, just as Spanish Humanism promoted a multicultural and multilingual approach to reading and writing, it also involved the creation of a culturally rich and historically continuous literary tradition in Spanish.

GRAMMATICAL NOTES

In spite of the remoteness of many aspects of Golden Age Spain's culture, the poems in this anthology deal with a variety of themes of relevance and interest to today's students. Nevertheless, one of the challenges in reading these poems is the use of archaic and non-standard grammar.

Assimilation

In Golden Age literature, an assimilation of consonants often occurs when the pronouns *lo, los, la, las, le,* and *les* follow an infinitive (**-rl- > -ll-**). These verses, from Lope de Vega's sonnet titled "Yo dije siempre, y lo diré, y lo digo," features assimilation by joining the verbs *ganar* and *perder* with the pronoun *le*:

Que no quiero ganalle / por no tener el miedo de perdelle

Contractions

The preposition *de* frequently contracts with pronouns such as *este, esta,* and *ella*. Also, as in modern Spanish, the word *de* combines with the article *el* in order to produce *del*, and the proposition *a* combines with *el* in order to produce *al*. In addition, *de* sometimes combines with the pronoun *él* in order to produce *dél*. You will encounter many instances of contraction in the poems in this collection. These verses, featuring the contraction *desto* (*de* + *esto*) come from the end of Garcilaso de la Vega's "Canción III":

> Quien tiene culpa desto / allá lo entenderás de mí muy presto

Enclitics

Sometimes pronouns were attached to the end of conjugated verbs; an attachment of this sort is known as an *enclitic*. These verses, from a sonnet by Cristóbal de Castillejo, makes the pronoun *les* an enclitic of the verb *parecieron*:

> Pareciéronles ser, como debía, / gentiles españoles caballeros

In modern Spanish the conjugated verb and the pronoun are usually separated, with the latter generally preceding the former. There are, however, instances of enclitic pronouns in modern Spanish. The following verses from the end of Castillejo's poem, featuring the enclitic construction *oyéndoles*, could pass as standard speech in today's world:

> Y oyéndoles hablar nuevo lenguaje / mezclado de extranjera poesía, / con ojos los miraban de extranjeros

Future Subjunctive

There used to be a future subjunctive in Spanish, but in modern Spanish the present subjunctive is used instead. The future subjunctive was formed like the past subjunctive in –ra-, but with an –e instead of an –a.

Though there are no consistent rules for translating the Spanish future subjunctive into English, the present tense—including use of the auxiliary "may"—usually conveys the meaning reasonably well. The following verses from Garcilaso de la Vega's "Canción III" feature the future subjunctive *quisiere*:

> El cuerpo está en poder / y en manos de quien puede / hacer a su placer lo que quisiere
> *My body is in the power and hands of someone who can do at his pleasure whatever he may wish*

"Haber de" + infinitive

The construction *haber de* may convey various meanings, but the most common in these poems include "must," "to be expected to," and "to be destined to." The following verse, from Garcilaso de la Vega's "Soneto V" ("Escrito está en mi alma vuestro gesto"), shows one meaning of the construction:

> Por vos he de morir, y por vos muero
> *For you I must die, and for you I am dying*

Past Subjunctive

In North America, when students study the past subjunctive, they usually only learn the forms that contain "r" in the inflection. For example: *saliera, comiéramos, pensaran, supieras*. These forms are common throughout Spanish America and in many parts of Spain. However, the past subjunctive also is expressed in a less common way, characterized by the presence of an "s" in the inflection. For example: *saliese, comiésemos, pensasen, supieses*. This version of the past subjunctive is considered more traditional, more classical, and more distinctively Castilian. These forms of the subjunctive are spoken in many parts of Spain (particularly in the north), and are standard in literary and journalistic discourse throughout the Hispanic world. During the Spanish Golden Age, this was the primary version of the past subjunctive in existence; the more common forms referred to above are more recent developments in the history of the language.

In these poems, you will come across many instances of the classical version of the past subjunctive. For example, the first verses of Juan Boscán's "Soneto I" read:

> Nunca de amor estuve tan contento / que en su loor mis versos ocupase
> *I was never so happy with love that I employed my verse in its praise*

The past subjunctive, especially the "r" form, was sometimes used in a way that conditionals are used today. These verses, for example, come from Garcilaso de la Vega's "Canción III." The "you" or *tú* that the speaker is addressing is the song or *canción* itself:

> Menos vida tuvieras / si hubiera de igualarte / con otras que se me han muerto en la boca
> *You would have a shorter life if I had to make you uniform in size with others* [i.e., other songs] *that have died on my mouth while they were spoken*

Present Subjunctive
Though students of Spanish tend to be familiar with the use of the present subjunctive in certain subordinate clauses, many students do not realize that the subjunctive may be used as the main verb in a main clause. The first two verses of Santa Teresa de Ávila's "Nada te turbe" provide a good example:

> Nada te turbe, / Nada te espante
> *Let nothing upset you, let nothing frighten you*

The speaker of these verses is issuing a kind of command, but instead of uttering a cumbersome sequence of clauses (such as *Es importante que nada te turbe*, or *No quiero que nada te espante*), the speaker chooses the high-impact simplicity as shown. In this case, the subject of the verb is in the third person ("nada"), and we can translate the verses using "let" or "may." This usage of subjunctive appears frequently in modern Spanish.

"Que" at the Beginning of Declarative Sentences
Students of Spanish tend to be quite familiar with "que"—really, "qué"—at the beginning of a question or exclamation: *¿Qué es eso? ¡Qué barbaridad!* Less familiar, however, is when "que" begins a regular, declarative sentence. These verses from Fray Luis de León's "Oda I" illustrate this phenomenon:

> Que no le enturbia el pecho / de los soberbios grandes el estado
> *The status of the proud noblemen does not trouble his breast*

The positioning of "que" at the beginning of a declarative sentence is, in fact, quite common in Spanish, especially in conversation. There is no exact translation for this usage in English, as the meaning depends on context. But when the verb following "que" is subjunctive, the sentence tends to carry significance as a command or wish. When the verb following "que" is indicative, the sentence tends to impart a sense of truth or certainty. Indeed, a good way to understand the meaning of a sentence beginning with "que" is to understand "que" as part of a larger, implied clause such as "es cierto que" or "es obvio que" (if the verb following "que" is indicative), or such as "quiero que" or "es importante que" (if the verb following "que" is subjunctive).

Ways of Saying "You" and "Your"
You will notice that Spanish Golden Age poetry uses a variety of words that mean "you" (subject or object pronoun). The most common of these, the singular *tú* and its variants (the direct/indirect object pronoun *te*, the prepositional object *ti*, and the possessive adjective *tu*), remains a standard form of address in Spain and in much of Spanish America. In Golden Age Spain, *tú* was generally used to address a child or social inferior, but it was also often used between intimate individuals.

Garcilaso de la Vega's "Canción V" as well as the poems by Santa Teresa de Ávila provide good examples of how *tú* is used in familiar, intimate discourse. The verb forms accompanying *tú* in these poems are the same as those in modern Spanish.

The singular pronoun *vos*, also common in these poems, was a respectful form of address that was generally used between social equals. Though less familiar and less intimate than *tú*, the use of *vos* did suggest some degree of familiarity between speaker and addressee. This helps to explain why in some dialects of modern Spanish (for example, in Argentina and in some parts of Central America), *vos* (and not *tú*) is the standard singular form of familiar address. However, the verb forms used with *vos* were not the same as those used with *tú*.

The plural pronoun *vosotros* (often rendered as "you all" in English) is also abundant in these poems. Indeed, in the Golden Age, *vosotros* functioned as the plural equivalent of the singular pronouns *vos* and *tú*. The verb forms accompanying *vosotros* (such as "sabéis" and "andáis") also accompanied the singular *vos*. The direct and indirect object pronoun for *vos* and *vosotros* was *os*, and the possessive adjective was *vuestro, vuestra*, etc. The command form for *vos* and *vosotros* (*dejad* for the infinitive *dejar*, for example) was the same as the command for *vosotros* today. Garcilaso de la Vega's "Soneto V" features the singular *vos* and its variants, while the same poet's "Soneto XI" uses the plural *vosotros* in various forms.

The poems in this anthology feature far fewer examples of formal terms of address. The pronoun *usted*, used in formal discourse today, appeared in written Spanish as early as 1620, but only gradually made its mark in poetry. Instead, lengthy and more elegant phrases were used in order to address social superiors. For example, Lope de Vega's burlesque sonnet "Quítenme aquesta puente que me mata" addresses the village councilmen as *señores regidores*. It is important to note that the accompanying verb forms for formal terms of address were the third-person singular and the third-person plural. In today's Spanish, the pronouns *usted* and *ustedes* (the formal terms of address for "you" and "you all") take the third-person verb forms. Indeed, the pronouns *usted* and *ustedes* derive from the phrases *Vuestra Merced* ("Your Grace") and *Vuestras Mercedes* ("Your Graces"), which were used with third-person verbs. Aside from *vuestro* (and the variants *vuestra, vuestros, vuestras*), other possessive adjectives meaning "your" in these poems include the formal *su* and *sus*, and the informal *tu* and *tus*.

VERSIFICATION

The word versification (*versificación*) refers to the form or metrical composition of poetry. In Golden Age poetry, each verse (*verso*) in a poem aims to consist of a predetermined number of syllables (*sílabas*), depending on the type or genre (*género*) of poem that the verse exists in. A sonnet (*soneto*) and a ballad (*romance*), for example, are specific genres of poem, and the conventions of these genres call for a specific number of syllables in each verse. In sonnets, each verse strives for eleven syllables, and in ballads, each verse strives for eight syllables.

Furthermore, many poems (such as sonnets) follow expectations with regard to how clusters of verses (that is, stanzas or *estrofas*) are arranged. The expectations for stanza formation generally have to do with rhyming patterns and number of verses. Some poems do not subdivide into stanzas, though (as in the case of ballads) rhyming patterns may still be present. The rhythm of sounds, the length of verses, the arrangement of verses into stanzas, the rhyming patterns, the total number of verses, and other techniques all affect a poem's musicality and lyricism. In order to appreciate this musicality and lyricism, including the meter (*metro*), rhythm (*ritmo*), and rhyme (*rima*) of a poem, we need to understand how sounds in poems are handled in order to meet expectations of syllable count (*cómputo silábico*).

Strong and Weak Vowels

Syllables are most often composed of vowel-consonant combinations, but a vowel alone can constitute its own independent syllable; for example, the "a" in "vamos a ganar" is the third syllable in the phrase. Sometimes two vowels combine to form what is known as a diphthong, which is two vowels joining up to form one syllable. For example, the word "bien" contains the diphthong "ie" and is considered to be a one-syllable word. However, the word "caos" contains two adjacent vowels, "ao", that do *not* form a diphthong; it is considered a two-syllable word. Why? While certain combinations of vowels form diphthongs, others do not. The vowels "a", "e", and "o" are all considered "strong" vowels, "vocales fuertes" in Spanish. When strong vowels are adjacent to each other (such as in the words "caos", "faena", and "roer") they do *not* form diphthongs. The vowels "i" ("y" after another vowel and at the end of the word, as in "hay", "hoy", "voy" etc.) and "u" are considered "weak" vowels, "vocales débiles" in Spanish. The only vowel combinations in Spanish that produce diphthongs are pairings of a weak vowel and a strong one, in either order (fuego, reina, necio, diablo, baile, cuota, hoy, voy, etc.) and the two weak vowels together, again in either order (ciudad, cuidado, ruido, etc). If there is an accent mark on the **weak** vowel of a strong-weak or weak-strong combination, the diphthong is considered broken, i.e., two syllables: día, filosofía, baúl, traído. However, if the accent falls on the **strong** vowel, its status as a diphthong is unaffected: andáis, coméis, canción, etc. If an accent falls on a diphthong created by two weak vowels, its status as a diphthong is also unaffected: "cuídate" is three syllables.

Possible diphthong pairings:
1. strong + weak
2. weak + strong
3. weak + weak

Accent marks with diphthong pairings:
In combinations containing a strong vowel, an accent on the weak vowel *breaks* the diphthong.
In combinations containing a strong vowel, an accent on the strong vowel *does not affect* the diphthong.
In combinations containing only weak vowels, an accent mark on either vowel *does not affect* the diphthong.

Flexibility in Counting Syllables

There are four types of license, or permission to stretch the rules, when it comes to counting syllables in a line: synalepha, synæresis, hiatus, and diæresis. Of the four, synalepha (see below) is considered normal and natural, the "default mode" of counting syllables. When you begin counting syllables in verses, you should assume that synalepha is in operation.

Aspects of Verse Length: Synalepha and Synæresis

The counting of syllables in poetry sometimes differs from how we usually count syllables. Each verse in a Golden Age poem is generally associated with a specific number of syllables, depending on the type of poem of which the verse is a part. Each verse in a *soneto* (sonnet), for example, has eleven syllables, such as this verse from Juan Boscán's Soneto I:

> según que por amar son infinitos
> *se-gún-que-por-a-mar-son-in-fi-ni-tos*

In the example above, the number of poetic syllables is equivalent to that of phonological syllables. In contrast, contiguous vowels usually blend together to form a single syllable. Here is an example, also from Boscán's Soneto I:

> que de este mal todo hombre se guardase
> *que-des-te-mal-to-d'hom-bre-se-guar-da-se*

In this example, thirteen phonological syllables are reduced to eleven poetic syllables, as *de este* is pronounced *deste*, and *todo hombre* is pronounced *tod'hombre*. This practice of blending vowel sounds between words is known as synalepha (*sinalefa*, in Spanish). Another, slightly more complicated example of synalepha may be seen in this example, also from the same poem:

buscando en el amor contentamiento
bus-can-doen-el-a-mor-con-ten-ta-mien-to

Thanks to synalepha, the twelve phonological syllables are reduced to eleven poetic syllables, as the *o* in *buscando* is combined with the *e* in *en*. By the way, it is important to note that the vowel sequence *ie* in *contentamiento* is a standard diphthong, and therefore is pronounced as part of a single syllable (*mien*, pronounced –myen-).

Synalepha is a common and powerful tool in composing poetry, but it also occurs regularly in spoken Spanish. For example, the pronunciation of the sentence "Ana está aquí" would sound very much like *A-naes-tá-quí*.

A similar method of combining vowel sounds in poetry is called synæresis (*sinéresis*, in Spanish). Whereas synalepha involves the blending of vowels between words, synæresis involves the blending, *within* a word, of two or more contiguous vowels that do not normally form a diphthong. An example is this verse from Fray Luis de León's Oda I:

El aire del huerto orea
El-ai-re-del-huer-to-rea

Whereas vowel combinations such as *ai* and *ue* are diphthongs (and thus pronounced as part of one syllable), the vowel sequence *ea*—two adjacent strong vowels—is not a diphthong in standard Spanish. (Phonologically, the word *orea* contains three syllables: *o-re-a*.) However, this verse is part of a *lira* (a poetic stanza made up of seven-syllable and eleven-syllable verses). In order to achieve the required seven syllables in this verse, the *e* and *a* must be blended to form a single sound. In effect, synæresis is used. Notice, in addition, that synalepha is used in order to combine the *o* sounds between the words *huerto* and *orea*.

Aspects of Verse Length: Hiatus and Diæresis
The terms synalepha and synæresis, which begin with the prefix *syn-*

(derived from a Greek word meaning "together with"), involve the joining together of vowel sounds in order to achieve a specific verse length in poetry. However, poets also use the technique of separating or dissociating vowel sounds in order to meet demands of verse length. One of these techniques, hiatus, is practice of separating vowel sounds between words that might otherwise be blended. A verse from San Juan de la Cruz's Canción I, a lengthy poem composed of seven-syllable and eleven-syllable verses, provides a good example:

> habiéndome herido
> *ha-bién-do-me-he-ri-do*

We might be tempted to combine the *e* sound of *me* and *herido* into one syllable, but in order to ensure the existence of seven poetic syllables in this verse, we may employ hiatus between the two words.

The practice of separating or disjoining vowel sounds *within* a word is termed diæresis—effectively, the opposite of synæresis. Typically, diæresis is used in order to separate the vowels that constitute a diphthong. For example, in the verse above, diæresis may be used to achieve seven poetic syllables if hiatus is not desired:

> habiéndome herido
> *ha-bi-én-do-mehe-ri-do*

With diæresis, the diphthong *ié* in *habiéndome* is dissociated, turning the word from four syllables to five. Another example of diæresis may be seen in a seven-syllable verse from Fray Luis de León's Oda I, a poem consisting of seven-syllable and eleven-syllable verses:

> con un manso ruido
> *con-un-man-so-ru-i-do*

Here, the need to pronounce separately the *u* and the *i* of *ruido* is clear: without diæresis, we have a six-syllable verse where we need a seven-syllable verse. In some other editions of Golden Age poetry the editors indicate the existence of diæresis by using an umlaut (two dots) over one of the separately pronounced vowels of a word. For example, in other texts, you may see *ruido* rendered as *rüido* or *ruïdo*. We have decided not to include this feature in this anthology so that you may explore diæresis on your own or in collaboration with your instructor.

Verse Endings and Counting of Syllables
In addition to the blending and separation of vowel sounds, there is another major feature in poetry that affects the number of syllables: the location of accent or stress at or near the end of the verse. Frequently, of the three final syllables in each verse, it is the next-to-last syllable (technically, the penultimate syllable, or *penúltima sílaba*) that receives the most stress. This kind of verse is called a *verso llano*. Here are examples from Garcilaso de la Vega's Soneto I and Canción V, respectively:

> Cuando me paro a contemplar mi es<u>ta</u>do
> *Cuan-do-me-pa-roa-con-tem-plar-mies-<u>ta</u>-do*

> Si de mi baja <u>li</u>ra
> *Si-de-mi-ba-ja-<u>li</u>-ra*

Though most of the verses in Golden Age poetry are *versos llanos*, you will also encounter verses in which the final stress falls on the very last syllable (*última sílaba*) and, very rarely, on the third-to-last syllable (*antepenúltima sílaba*).

When the stress at the end of a verse falls on the final syllable, the verse is a *verso agudo*. In the computation of syllables in a *verso agudo*, a phantom syllable is added to those already counted. This is because, as the final word ends with stress on the final syllable, this syllable is sounded with special intensity and a brief pause is needed. The following *versos agudos* come from Sor Juana Inés de la Cruz's "Hombres necios que acusáis," a lengthy poem consisting of eight-syllable verses:

Hombres necios que acusáis
Hom-bres-ne-cios-quea-cu-sáis-[+1]
a la mujer sin razón
a-la-mu-jer-sin-ra-zón-[+1]
sin ver que sois la ocasión
sin-ver-que-sois-lao-ca-sión-[+1]
de lo mismo que culpáis.
de-lo-mis-mo-que-cul-páis-[+1]

In this anthology you will not encounter examples of verses in which stress falls on the third-to-last syllable. These verses—called *versos esdrújulos*—are rare, but it is nonetheless important to recognize them.

Arte mayor and arte menor

Verses in Spanish containing eight or fewer syllables are classified as *arte menor*. Verses containing nine or more syllables are considered *arte mayor*. Typically, as poems in *arte menor* tend to reflect comical and popular themes, poems in *arte mayor* tend to reflect serious themes, including philosophical matters. Sometimes poems combine verses in *arte menor* with verses in *arte mayor*; these poems tend to be meditative and deal with serious themes.

Aspects of Rhyme: Assonance and Consonance

In most poems of the Spanish Golden Age, the final two syllables of a verse correspond in sound to the final two syllables of at least one other nearby verse. This sound similarity is known as rhyme (*rima*), and there are two kinds of end-verse rhyme: full rhyme (*rima consonante*) and assonant rhyme (*rima asonante*).

Full rhyme occurs when there is a pairing of verses whose endings, from the stress on, are identical. In effect, the vowel sounds as well as the consonant sounds in the final two syllables of such verses are equivalent. In Garcilaso de la Vega's Soneto I ("Cuando me paro a contemplar mi estado"), for example, full rhyme is achieved in the first stanza with the pairs *estado-llegado* and *traído-perdido*.

Assonant rhyme occurs when there is a pairing of verses whose endings, from the stress on, are identical in the vowel sounds only. In effect, the consonants in the final two syllables of such verses may vary, because the vowel sounds carry the rhyme. Sor Juana Inés de la Cruz's *A la Encarnación* demonstrates this phenomenon.

Rhyme Scheme Notation
In order to express a poem's rhyme scheme, a notation system using upper-case and lowercase letters of the alphabet (*ABAB, aBabB*, etc.) is commonly used. When a verse is in *arte menor*, the rhyme is symbolically represented by a small letter; when a verse is in *arte mayor*, the rhyme is symbolically represented by a large letter. Each distinct rhyme is assigned a letter, beginning with *a* or *A*. For example, the rhyme scheme for the first stanza of Fray Luis de León's "Oda III" is as follows:

El aire se serena	*a*
y viste de hermosura y luz no usada,	*B*
Salinas, cuando suena	*a*
la música extremada,	*b*
por vuestra sabia mano gobernada.	*B*

This stanza, an example of a *lira* (see below), consists of three seven-syllable verses as well as two eleven-syllable verses, arranged in a specific order. This stanza also features two rhyme systems, "-ena" and "-ada," also arranged in a specific order. The notation system, in effect, illustrates the two dimensions (verse length and rhyme) at play in the stanza. The two verses indicated by *a* have the same syllable count (seven) and rhyme ("-ena"); the two verses indicated by *B* have matching syllable counts (eleven) and a distinct rhyme correspondence ("-ada"). And the verse marked *b* shares the syllable count (seven) of verses designated by *a*, but contains the rhyme ("-ada") of the verses indicated by *B*. In the description of poetic forms and genres below, we have provided rhyme schemes for some of the more common categories of poem. However, many poetic genres (such as sonnets) contain a variety of rhyme schemes, so it is a good idea to determine on your own the rhyme scheme of each particular poem that you encounter.

Poetic Forms and Genres

There are many different kinds of poetic forms and genres in Golden Age poetry, and many of them are represented in this anthology.

CANCIÓN

A *canción* is a poetic composition with stanzas containing alternating verses of seven and eleven syllables. The number of stanzas, the number of verses in each stanza, and the exact arrangement of verses according to length and rhyme, vary widely. Garcilaso de la Vega's "Canción III," for example, consists of six stanzas: five of them contain thirteen verses each, with the eleven-syllable verses consistently appearing in third, sixth, eleventh, and thirteenth place; the rhyme scheme for each of these stanzas is *abCabCcdeeDfF*. The sixth stanza contains eight verses, with the eleven-syllable verses appearing third, sixth, and eighth; the rhyme scheme is *abCabCdD*. In contrast, Fray Luis de León's "Canción III" consists of four stanzas, each containing six verses. The eleven-syllable verses appear in the third and sixth position of each stanza, and the rhyme scheme is *abCabC*.

Garcilaso's "Canción V" began a specific poetic subgenre known as the *lira*, so named because of the first verse of his poem: "Si de mi baja lira..." As the poem itself shows, the *lira* is a stanza of five verses in the rhyme scheme *aBabB*, with the seven-syllable verses in the first, third, and fourth position, and the eleven-syllable verses in the second and fifth position. Many other Golden Age poets cultivated the *lira*, including Fray Luis de León in his "Canción II."

DÉCIMA

The *décima* is a stanza form consisting of ten verses, with each verse containing eight syllables. The rhyme scheme for a *décima* is *abbaaccddc*. In this anthology, *décimas* from Pedro Calderón de la Barca's famous play *La vida es sueño* are featured.

LETRILLA

A *letrilla* is a kind of light poem containing short stanzas, with each stanza usually ending with a refrain. Many, though certainly not all, *letrillas* are satirical. *Letrillas* by Luis de Góngora and Francisco de Quevedo are featured in this anthology.

OCTAVA REAL

An *octava real* contains eight verses, and each verse contains eleven syllables. The rhyme scheme for an *octava real* is *ABABABCC*. In this anthology, two *octavas reales* from Alonso de Ercilla's epic *La Araucana* have been included.

OVILLEJO

An *ovillejo* is a stanza consisting of ten verses whose rhyme scheme is *aa bb cc cddc*. Though the first six verses form three rhyming pairs, the first verse in each pair is a question eight syllables in length, and the second verse in each pair is a one- or two-word response of three syllables. The final four verses of an *ovillejo* are a *redondilla* (see below). Miguel de Cervantes, believed to have written the first *ovillejos*, is the author of the only *ovillejo* included in this anthology.

REDONDILLA

A *redondilla* is a poetic unit of four verses, each containing eight syllables. Rhyme is usually full and follows the *abba* pattern. Though *redondillas* tend to be associated more closely with Golden Age drama, many fine examples of *redondillas* exist in lyric poetry. In this anthology, Sor Juana's "Hombres necios que acusáis" is a well-known poem consisting of seventeen *redondillas*.

ROMANCE

A *romance*, or ballad, is a song consisting of eight-syllable verses. The *romance*'s origins in oral culture come through in the rhyme scheme: the rhyme is assonant (vocalic) and occurs on the even-numbered verses. The odd-numbered verses in *romances* do not rhyme, so the rhyme scheme is often depicted as *0a0a0a0a*, with the zero (0) representing lack of rhyme. Generally speaking, *romances* are fairly simple and easy to remember. They can range in length from four verses to incredibly long compositions. Indeed, medieval epics consist partly or entirely of *romances*. In this collection, the only *romance* featured is Sor Juana Inés de la Cruz's *A la Encarnación*.

SONETO

The sonnet is by far the most represented poetic genre in this anthology, and for good reason: many of the greatest masterpieces of Spanish Golden Age poetry are sonnets. Golden Age sonnets consist of fourteen verses, divided into two quatrains (*cuartetos*—stanzas containing four verses) and two tercets (*tercetos*—stanzas containing three verses). Each verse contains eleven syllables. The rhyme is full (*rima consonante*) and may be organized in a variety of ways. For example, the rhyme scheme for Juan Boscán's "Soneto I" is *ABBA ABBA CDC CDC*, but the rhyme scheme for Garcilaso de la Vega's "Soneto XXIII" is *ABBA ABBA CDE DCE*. This anthology also features sonnets by Cristóbal de Castillejo, Miguel de Cervantes, Luis de Góngora, Lope de Vega, Francisco de Quevedo, and Sor Juana Inés de la Cruz.

WORKS CONSULTED

Though we have consulted dozens of studies for our introduction, biographies, and footnotes, the following have figured most prominently. In addition, the full bibliographical information for the texts that we cite may be found in this list. You may find some of these texts helpful for further study of the culture, history, and poetry of Golden Age Spain:

Alonso, Dámaso. *Poesía española. Ensayo de métodos y límites estilísticos. Garcilaso, Fray Luis de León, San Juan de la Cruz, Góngora, Lope de Vega, Quevedo*. Madrid: Gredos, 1957

Arenal, Electa and Amanda Powell, eds. and trans. *The Answer / La Respuesta*. New York: Feminist Press, 1994

Barrett, Linton Lomas. *Five Centuries of Spanish Literature*. Long Grove, Ill.:

Waveland, 2003

Bataillon, Marcel. *Erasmo y España: Estudios sobre la historia espiritual del siglo XVI.* México: Fondo de Cultura Económica, 1950

Baudot, Georges. "La trova náhuatl de Sor Juana Inés de la Cruz." *Estudios de folkore y literatura dedicados a Mercedes Díaz Roig.* pp. 849-59. Ed. Beatriz Garza Guarón and Yvette Jiménez de Báez. México: Colegio de México, 1992

Elliott, John H. *Imperial Spain, 1469-1716.* London: Penguin, 1970

Kamen, Henry. *How Spain Became a World Power, 1492-1763.* London: Perennial, 2004

Kavanaugh, Kieran, and Otilio Rodríguez, eds. and trans. *The Collected Works of St. John of the Cross.* Washington, D.C.: ICS Publications, 1991

McCaw, R. John, ed. *El burlador de Sevilla.* By Tirso de Molina. Newark, Del.: Cervantes and Co., 2003

Moore, Roger. "Erase un hombre a una nariz pegado. The Enigma of the Second Tercet." *Romance Quarterly* 42.1 (1995): 39-46

Rivers, Elias L. "Diglossia in New Spain." *University of Dayton Review.* 16.2 (1983): 9-12

———. *Poesía lírica del Siglo de Oro.* Madrid: Cátedra, 1987

———, ed. *Renaissance and Baroque Poetry of Spain with English Prose Translations.* Prospect Heights, Ill.: Waveland, 1988

Virgillo, Carmelo, Edward H. Friedman, and L. Teresa Valdivieso, eds. *Aproximaciones al estudio de la literatura hispánica.* 4th ed. Boston: McGraw Hill College, 1999

Wardropper, Bruce. *Spanish Poetry of the Golden Age.* New York: Appleton-Century-Crofts, 1971

SELECTED BIBLIOGRAPHY

Though you will find titles of recommended texts related to specific poets in the biographies, you also may find the following texts helpful in providing further general knowledge about the culture, history, and poetry of Golden Age Spain:

Collard, Andrée M. *Nueva poesía; conceptismo, culteranismo en la crítica española.* Madrid: Castalia, 1967

Cruz, Anne J. *Imitación y transformación: el petrarquismo en la poesía de Boscán y Garcilaso de la Vega.* Amsterdam and Philadelphia: Benjamins, 1988

Elliott, John H. *Spain and Its World, 1500-1700: Selected Essays.* New Haven: Yale

UP, 1989

Navarrete, Ignacio. *Orphans of Petrarch: Poetry and Theory in the Spanish Renaissance*. Berkeley: U of California P, 1994

Terry, Arthur. *Seventeenth-Century Spanish Poetry: The Power of Artifice*. Cambridge and New York: Cambridge UP, 1993

Juan Boscán (ca. 1490-1542)

JUAN BOSCÁN ALMOGÁVER, A Catalonian from Barcelona, is also known by his name in Catalan: Joan Boscà i Almogàver. He was a courtier and friend of Garcilaso de la Vega, who is also featured in this anthology; they fought together against the invading Turks in Rhodes. Though Boscán was among the first to write Italianate poetry ("poesía italianizante") in Castilian, he—along with the Venetian ambassador Andrea Navagero (Navaggiero in Italian)—is credited with encouraging Garcilaso to take up the Italian style of verse writing in Spanish. After Garcilaso's death in 1536, Boscán organized and edited his friend's poetry for publication.

Boscán's own death in 1542 prevented him from seeing the publication of Garcilaso's verse during his lifetime, but his widow Ana Girón de Rebolledo published this work, along with Boscán's own poetry, in *Las obras de Boscán y algunas de Garcilaso de la Vega* (Barcelona, 1543). Boscán's other great contribution to Renaissance Spain was his translation into Spanish of the Italian Baldassare Castiglione's *The Book of the Courtier* (1534), which described the characteristics of the ideal courtier and was a model of elegant writing. Boscán also translated the poetry of Ausiàs March, the first great poet to write in Catalan, into Spanish.

Darst, David. *Juan Boscán*. Boston: Twayne, 1978.

SONETO I

Nunca de amor estuve tan contento
que en su loor° mis versos° ocupase°[1]   *praise, poetry, I employed*
ni a nadie consejé° que se engañase,   **aconsejé** = *I advised*
buscando en el amor contentamiento.°[2]   *contentment*

5   Esto siempre juzgó° mi entendimiento:°   *judged, rational mind*
que de este mal° todo hombre se guardase.°   *evil, guard against*
Y así, porque° esta ley se conservase,   **para que**
'holgué de ser° a todos escarmiento.°[3]   *I was happy to be, lesson*

¡Oh! vosotros que 'andáis tras° mis escritos   *follow*
10 gustando de leer tormentos° tristes   *torments*
'según que por amar° son infinitos,   *which because of love*

Mis versos son deciros: "¡Oh, benditos°   *blessed*
los que de Dios tan gran merced° hubistes°   *mercy, have received*
que del poder de amor fuésedes° quitos!°[4]   *you were, freed*

---

[1] **Nunca de amor...** *I was never so happy with love that I employed my verse in its praise*

[2] **Ni a nadie...** *Nor did I ever advise any man to deceive himself by seeking happiness in love*

[3] **Esto siempre juzgó...** *I always judged that every man should guard himself against this evil. And so in order that this law be preserved, I enjoyed serving as a warning for everybody else*

[4] **Benditos los que...** *Blessed are you who have received such great mercy from God that you were freed from the power of love*

SONETO LXI

Dulce soñar y dulce congojarme,°   self-affliction
cuando estaba soñando que soñaba;[5]
dulce gozar° con lo que me engañaba,   enjoyment
si un poco más durara° el engañarme;°[6]   might have lasted, self-deception

5   Dulce no 'estar en mí,°[7] que figurarme°   to be rational, to imagine
podía cuanto° bien° yo deseaba,[8]   how much
dulce placer,° aunque 'me importunaba°   joy, it bothered me
que 'alguna vez° llegaba a despertarme.[9]   at times

¡Oh sueño, cuánto más leve° y sabroso°   light, delightful
10   'me fueras° si vinieras tan pesado°   you would be to me, heavy
que asentaras° en mí con más reposo!°[10]   settled, tranquility

Durmiendo, en fin, fui bienaventurado,°   blessed
y es justo° en la mentira ser dichoso°   fair, blissful
quien siempre en la verdad fue desdichado.°[11]   miserable

---

[5] **Dulce soñar...** *How sweet it was to dream and how sweet it was to be afflicted, when I was dreaming that I was dreaming.* The poet here is referring to the thrill of being in love, even when such an experience produces suffering.

[6] **Dulce gozar...** *How sweet it was to take pleasure in what was deceiving me, if only my self-deception could have lasted a bit longer*

[7] **Dulce no estar...** *How sweet it was not to be in my right mind*

[8] **Figurarme...** *I was able to imagine all the good I desired*

[9] **Alguna vez...** *It would at times bring me to the point of awakening*

[10] **¡Oh sueño...** *Oh sleep, how much lighter and more pleasant you would be for me if you came so heavy as to settle in me with more tranquility!* Note in this poem how the word "sueño" is used to mean both "dream" and "sleep."

[11] **Es justo...** *It is only just that one who was always made miserable by the truth should be made blissful by a lie*

Garcilaso de la Vega (ca. 1501-1536)

GARCILASO DE LA VEGA LIVED a short, intense, productive life. His poetic output is small but of the highest quality, and influenced generations of Spanish poets who still look to him as one of the greatest of their tradition.

Garcilaso was born into the highest levels of the Spanish aristocracy. He was educated for life as a courtier and soldier of the empire. With the Spanish Reconquest of Muslim Granada completed in 1492, Garcilaso was born and raised in a cultural milieu in which the aristocracy had the time and resources to pursue intellectual as well as military activities. Garcilaso's education took place in a new historical context: the Humanist movement, which advocated a revival of classical learning. The sons of the nobility started to learn Latin and Greek and read classical literature in the original languages. Once mastered, Latin was the language of instruction in the Liberal Arts curriculum. Garcilaso showed his mastery of Latin by writing excellent verse in that language.

One of the most important individuals who contributed to this educational movement that formed Garcilaso was Antonio de Nebrija, sometimes written "Lebrija." (1444-1533). Nebrija's impact on Spanish education cannot be overstated. He had studied at the University of Bologna and taught at the University of Salamanca, thereby importing the Humanist approaches from Italy to Spain. In addition to his bilingual dictionaries, he wrote the *Gramática sobre la lengua castellana* (Salamanca, 1492). This work was not only the first grammar manual of Spanish ever produced, it was also the first one of any European language other than classical Greek and Latin ever published. This grammar was a great step forward in establishing the validity of Spanish as a linguistic instrument that could produce literary masterpieces. Indeed, Garcilaso's elegant and polished verse in Castilian was felt to be the equal of Latin poetry, and Nebrija's writings helped pave the way for a new change in attitude towards poetry written in the vernacular.

Garcilaso's other important cultural influence was Italian poetry; Italy was the center of the new wave of learning. Cultivated gentlemen at the court of Charles V such as Juan Boscán and Garcilaso cast aside older, traditional forms of Spanish poetry for newer forms: the sonnet, the *canción*, the *lira*, the eclogue. Garcilaso and Boscán were inspired to try these new forms by a conversation with Andrea Navagero, the Venetian ambassador to the court of Charles V. These new poetic styles were referred to in their time as "poesía italianizante," that is, poetry in the Italian style.

Garcilaso was a highly respected soldier and courtier. He was dubbed a knight of the Order of Santiago and made a highly advantageous marriage with Charles V's approval and sponsorship. He greatly displeased the emperor, however, by his presence at the nuptials of his nephew. All marriages between nobles had to be approved by the sovereign, and this one had taken place, it seemed, specifically to pre-empt the possibility of his disapproval. For his participation, Garcilaso was exiled to an island in the Danube river and afterwards was ordered to Naples, then under Spanish power. It is in this latter location where it is thought he composed his greatest works. He was killed in battle in France in service to the king in 1536.

Fernández-Morera, Dario. *The Lyre and the Oaten Flute: Garcilaso and the Pastoral.* London: Tamesis, 1982

Gicovate, Bernard. *Garcilaso de la Vega.* Boston: Twayne, 1975

Rivers, Elias. *Garcilaso de la Vega: Poems: A Critical Guide.* London: Grant and Cutler, 1980

SONETO I

Cuando 'me paro° a contemplar mi estado°   I pause, condition
y a ver los pasos° por do° me ha traído,   steps, **donde**
hallo, según por do anduve perdido,
que a 'mayor mal° pudiera haber llegado.[1]   worse situation

5   Mas° cuando del camino estó° olvidado,°   But, **estoy**, oblivious
a tanto mal no sé por do he venido.[2]
Sé que 'me acabo,° y más, he yo sentido   I die
ver acabar° comigo mi cuidado.°   end, suffering

Yo acabaré, que 'me entregué° 'sin arte°   I gave in, carelessly
10 a quien° sabrá perderme° y acabarme,   someone who, destroy me
si ella quisiere. Y aun° sabrá querello.°[3]   yet, **quererlo**

'Que pues° mi voluntad puede matarme,   For since
la suya, que no es tanto 'de mi parte,°   in my favor
pudiendo,° ¿qué hará, si no hacello?°[4]   having the power, **hacerlo**

---

[1] **Hallo...** *I find that, given where I walked astray, I could have ended up in a worse situation*

[2] **Mas cuando...** *But when I am oblivious of the road, I do not know how I have arrived at such misfortune*

[3] **Y aun...** *And she will yet wish to [destroy me].*

[4] **Que pues...** *For since my will can kill me, hers, which is not so much in my favor, having the power to do so.... What else will it do if not kill me?*

SONETO V

    Escrito está en mi alma vuestro° gesto,°   your, face
y cuanto yo escrevir° de vos deseo;[5]   **escribir**
Vos sola lo escrevistes, yo lo leo
tan solo que aun de vos 'me guardo° en esto.   I keep my distance

5   En esto estoy, y estaré siempre puesto;
que aunque no cabe en mí cuanto en vos veo,
de tanto bien lo que no entiendo creo,
tomando ya la fe 'por presupuesto.°[6]   as a given

    Yo no nací sino para quereros;[7]
10 mi alma os ha cortado a su medida,°[8]   size
por hábito° del alma misma os quiero.[9]   custom

    Cuanto tengo confieso yo deberos.[10]
por vos nací, por vos tengo la vida;
por vos he de morir, y por vos muero.

---

[5] **Y cuanto...** *And all that I wish to write about you*

[6] **De tanto bien...** *I believe what I do not understand of such goodness, ever taking faith as a given*

[7] **Yo no nací...** *I was only born to love you*

[8] **Mi alma...** *My soul has tailored you to its size*

[9] The word "hábito" also refers to an article of clothing.

[10] **Cuanto tengo...** *I confess that I owe you what I have*

SONETO XI

Hermosas ninfas°[11] que, en el río metidas,°
contentas habitáis° en las moradas°
de relucientes° piedras fabricadas,
y en colunas de vidro° sostenidas;°[12]

5   Agora estéis labrando° embebecidas,°[13]
o tejiendo° las telas° delicadas;
agora unas con otras apartadas,°
contándoos° los amores y las vidas;

Dejad un rato° la labor alzando°
10 vuestras rubias° cabezas a mirarme,
y 'no os detendréis mucho,° según ando.

Que o no podréis de lástima° escucharme,
o convertido° en agua aquí llorando
podréis allá 'de espacio° consolarme.[14]

nymphs, immersed
you live, dwellings
shining
vidrio *= glass, supported*

embroidering, occupied
weaving, cloths
set apart in small groups
telling each other

while, raising
blonde
it won't take much time

pity
transformed
for a while

---

[11] In classical mythology, nymphs are minor deities represented as beautiful maidens inhabiting natural places such as rivers, forests, and the sea.

[12] **De relucientes...** *Built from shining rocks and supported by glass columns*

[13] **Agora estéis...** *At this moment you may be occupied with embroidering...* The verb "estéis" is auxiliary to the gerunds "labrando," "tejiendo," and "contando."

[14] The speaker offers the nymphs two options by using "o...o..." (*"either...or..."*).

SONETO XXIII

'En tanto que° de rosa y azucena°   While, lily
se muestra la color en vuestro° gesto,°¹⁵   your, face
y que° vuestro mirar° ardiente,° honesto°   = *en tanto* **que**, gaze, burning, chaste
enciende° al corazón y lo refrena;°   inflame, restrains

5   Y en tanto que el cabello,¹⁶ que en la vena°   mineral vein
del oro 'se escogió,°¹⁷ con vuelo° presto°   was composed, flutter, quick
por el hermoso cuello, blanco, enhiesto°   upright
el viento mueve, esparce° y desordena;°   scatters, disorders

Coged° de vuestra alegre primavera°   Gather, youth
10 el dulce fruto, que el tiempo airado°   angry
cubra de nieve la hermosa cumbre.°¹⁸   mountain top

Marchitará° la rosa el viento helado,°¹⁹   will destroy, icy
todo lo mudará° 'la edad ligera,°²⁰   will change, fleeting time
por no hacer mudanza° en su costumbre   change

---

¹⁵ **En tanto que...** *While the colors of roses and lilies linger in your face*
¹⁶ The word "cabello" is the direct object of the stanza; the subject is "viento," and the verbs are "mueve, esparce y desordena."
¹⁷ **Que en la vena...** *Which was assembled from gold from the earth's veins*
¹⁸ **Que el tiempo airado...** *For angry Time may cover the lovely mountain top with snow*
¹⁹ **Marchitará...** *The icy wind will destroy the rose*
²⁰ **Todo...** *Fleeting time will change everything*

CANCION III

    Con un manso° ruido   gentle
de agua corriente y clara
cerca el Danubio°²¹ una isla, que pudiera   Danube River
ser lugar escogido,
5 para que descansara
quien, como yo estó agora, no estuviera;²²
do siempre primavera
parece en la verdura
'sembrada de° las flores,   sown with
10 hacen los ruiseñores°   nightingales
renovar° el placer,° o la tristura°²³   renew, joy, sadness
con sus blandas° querellas,°   soft, complaints
que nunca día ni noche 'cesan dellas.°²⁴   end them

    Aquí estuve yo puesto°   placed
15 o, por mejor decillo,
preso° y forzado° y solo en tierra ajena.°   imprisoned, constrained, foreign
Bien° pueden hacer esto   Well
en quien puede sufrillo,
y en quien él a sí mismo se condena.
20 Tengo sólo una pena:°
si muero desterrado°   sorrow
y en tanta desventura,°   in exile
                                     misfortune

---

²¹ **Cerca el Danubio una isla...** *The Danube surrounds an island.* The Danube is a river in south-central Europe. In 1531, Garcilaso attended his nephew's secret marriage to a lady for whom Charles V (the Holy Roman Emperor, also King Charles I of Spain) had other plans. Due to a misunderstanding of Garcilaso's role in this marriage, the Emperor exiled him to an island in the Danube. After six months there, the exile was commuted to Naples.

²² **Para que descansara...** *For someone, not in the condition I'm in, to rest*

²³ **Hacen los ruiseñores...** *The nightingales provoke the renewal of joy or sadness.* The nightingale is a European songbird. The male nightingale is known for his melodic song during courtship.

²⁴ The subject of the verb "cesan" is "ruiseñores."

que piensen 'por ventura,°   by chance
que juntos tantos males me han llevado.
25 Y sé yo bien que muero
por sólo aquello que morir espero.[25]

El cuerpo está en poder
y en manos de quien puede
hacer a su placer lo que quisiere.[26]
30 Mas no podrá hacer   I end up the worse for wear
que 'mal librado quede,°   any other form of control, does not
mientras de mí 'otra prenda° 'no tuviere.°[27]   bad ending
Cuando ya el mal° viniere   final, fate
y la postrera° suerte,°
35 aquí me ha de hallar
en el mismo lugar.[28]
Que otra cosa más dura que la muerte
me halla y ha hallado,
y esto sabe muy bien quien lo ha probado.°[29]   experienced

40 No es necesario agora
hablar más 'sin provecho,°   for naught
que es mi necesidad muy apretada.°   urgent
Pues ha sido en una hora
todo aquello deshecho°   undone
45 en que toda mi vida fue gastada.
¡Y al fin de tal jornada°   expedition

---

[25] **Y sé yo...** *And I know well that I'm dying for that alone for which I hope to die*

[26] **El cuerpo está en poder...** *My body is in the power and hands of someone who can do at his pleasure whatever he may wish.* The "someone" referred to here is Emperor Charles V.

[27] The subject of the verbs "podrá" and "tuviere" is "quien," from verse 28. The subject of "quede" is "yo."

[28] The subject of "ha de hallar" is "mal," from verse 33.

[29] **Y esto sabe muy bien...** *And the person who has experienced it [i.e., the "otra cosa más dura que la muerte"] knows this very well*

'presumen espantarme!°   they think they can scare me
Sepan, que ya no puedo
morir, si no sin miedo.
50 Que aun nunca que temer quiso dejarme
la desventura mía
que el bien° y el miedo me quitó en un día.   contentment

Danubio, río divino,
que por fieras° naciones   fierce
55 vas con tus claras ondas° discurriendo;°   waves, flowing
pues no hay otro camino
'por donde° mis razones°   whereby, words
vayan fuera de aquí, si no corriendo[30]
por tus aguas, y siendo
60 en ellas anegadas.°   drowned
Si en tierra tan ajena°   alien
en la desierta arena°   sand
fueren de alguno° acaso° en fin halladas,[31]   someone, by chance
entiérrelas siquiera,°[32]   if you please
65 porque su error se acabe en tu ribera.°[33]   shore

Aunque en el agua mueras,
Canción, no has de quejarte,
que yo he mirado° bien 'lo que te toca.°   considered, what is coming to you
Menos° vida tuvieras,   shorter
70 si hubiera de igualarte°   make you uniform in size
con otras° que se me han muerto en la boca.[34] = otras *canciones*

---

[30] The subject of the gerund "corriendo" is "mis razones."

[31] **Si en tierra...** *If in such alien land, on the desert sand, they ["mis razones"] are by chance and at last found by another*

[32] The subject of "entiérrelas" is "alguno."

[33] The possessive "su" refers to "razones"; the possessive "tu" refers to the Danube, to which the poetic voice is speaking

[34] **Menos vida tuvieras...** *You would have a shorter life if I had to cut you to the same length as those [other songs] that have died in my mouth while they were spoken*

Quien tiene culpa° desto,   blame

allá lo entenderás° de mí muy presto.°   you will hear, soon

CANCION V

Si de mi baja° lira°
'tanto pudiese° el son,°[35] que en un momento
aplacase° la ira°
del animoso° viento,
5   y la furia del mar y el movimiento;[36]

lowly, lyre
could have so much power, sou~
it could calm, anger
energetic

Y en ásperas° montañas
con el suave canto enterneciese°
las fieras° alimañas;°
los árboles moviese,
10 y al son confusamente los trajese.°[37]

rough
it could tame
wild, beasts

could carry them

'No pienses que cantado
sería de mí, hermosa flor de Nido,[38]
el fiero Marte airado,[39]

---

[35] The noun "son" is the subject of the verbs "pudiese" and "aplacase," and is also the subject of the verbs in the following stanza.

[36] The words "ira," "furia," and "movimiento" are direct objects of the verb "aplacase."

[37] The noun "son" from the first stanza is the subject of the verbs "enterneciese," "moviese," and "trajese."

[38] The phrase "flor de Nido," sometimes rendered "flor de Gnido," has more than one possible meaning. Knidos (also rendered as "Cnidus") was an ancient Greek city in what is now modern-day Turkey. Among the many important sites at Knidos was a temple dedicated to Aphrodite, the ancient Greek goddess of love and beauty that came to be known as Venus in Roman culture. The Flower of Knidos, then, would be Aphrodite herself. The "flor de Nido" also may refer to a specific woman and acquaintance of Garcilaso's, Violante Sanseverino, from the Nido section of the southern Italian city of Naples. Mario Galeota, a friend of Garcilaso's, fell in love with this woman, but she did not show interest in return. Some believe that Garcilaso wrote this poem in order to sway Violante in favor of his friend; others believe that this poem reveals Garcilaso's own interest in Violante. This poem is often referred to as "Oda a la flor de Nido."

[39] **No pienses...** *Don't think, beautiful flower of Nido, that wild, angry Mars would be sung by me.* In Roman mythology, Mars is the god of war.

a muerte convertido,°   attuned
15 de polvo° y sangre y de sudor° teñido;°⁴⁰   dust, sweat, stained

    Ni aquellos capitanes,
en las sublimes° ruedas° colocados,°   lofty, chariot wheels, positioned
por quien° los alemanes   = *Marte*
el fiero cuello atados,°   bound
20 y los franceses van domesticados.°⁴¹   conquered

    Mas solamente aquella°   that
fuerza° de tu beldad sería cantada;   power
y 'alguna vez° con ella°   on occasion, = *aquella fuerza*
también sería notada
25 el aspereza° de que estás armada.⁴²   cruelty

    Y cómo por ti sola
y por tu gran valor y hermosura,
convertido en viola,°   violet flower
llora su desventura
30 el miserable amante° en su figura.°⁴³   lover, bodily form

    Hablo de aquel cativo°   *cautivo* = captive
de quien tenerse debe más cuidado,°⁴⁴   care
que está muriendo vivo,
al remo° condenado,°   oar, condemned

---

⁴⁰ These last two verses describe the god Mars.

⁴¹ The phrase from the previous stanza, "No pienses que cantado/ sería de mí," leads into this stanza, as well.

⁴² The cruelty of a beloved lady is an important theme in Renaissance literature.

⁴³ The theme of metamorphosis is also very popular in Renaissance literature. In this case, the male lover has transformed into a violet.

⁴⁴ **Hablo...** *I speak of that captive, to whom one ought to be more attentive....* Another popular theme in Renaissance poetry is that of the male lover as a captive of his beloved lady. Frequently, the lady is indifferent or disdainful of the man who feels captivated by her.

35 en la concha° de Venus amarrado.°⁴⁵   shell, tied down

Por ti, 'como solía,°   like he used to
del áspero° caballo 'no corrige°   untamed, he does not control
la furia y gallardía;°   intensity
ni con freno° lo rige,°⁴⁶   bit, controls
40 ni con vivas espuelas° ya lo aflige.°⁴⁷   spurs, hurt

Por ti con diestra° mano   skillful
no revuelve° la espada presurosa;°   wield, swift
y en el dudoso° llano°   doubtful, plain
huye la polvorosa°   dusty
45 palestra,° como sierpe° ponzoñosa.°⁴⁸   fray, snake, poisonous

Por ti su blanda° musa,⁴⁹   tender
en lugar de la cítara° sonante,°   zither, sounding
tristes querellas° usa,   complaints
que con llanto abundante
50 hacen bañar el rostro del amante.⁵⁰

Por ti el mayor amigo
le es importuno,° grave° y enojoso;°   annoying, grievous, bothersome

---

⁴⁵ In late Roman mythology, Venus was the goddess of love and beauty. In Renaissance art and literature, she is often depicted as standing in her conch shell, a symbol of her birth and emergence from the seas. The adjective "amarrado" refers to the lover (the "cativo"), not to Venus or her shell.

⁴⁶ A "freno" here refers to a "bit," which is the mouthpiece of a bridled horse.

⁴⁷ The "cativo" from the previous stanza is the subject of the verbs "corrige," "rige," and "aflige."

⁴⁸ The "cativo" is the subject of the verbs in this stanza.

⁴⁹ In Greek mythology, each of the nine Muses is a patron goddess for a specific art or science. The word "muse" in general refers to a source of inspiration.

⁵⁰ The noun "musa" is the subject of the verb "usa," and the direct object is "tristes querellas."

yo puedo ser testigo,°   witness
que ya del peligroso
55 naufragio° fui su puerto y su reposo.[51]   shipwreck

Y agora en tal manera
vence° el dolor a la razón perdida,[52]   triumphs
que ponzoñosa° fiera°   poisonous, beast
nunca fue aborrecida°   hated
60 tanto, como yo de él, ni tan temida.[53]

No fuiste tú engendrada°   conceived
ni producida° de la dura tierra;   born
no debe ser notada
que ingratamente° yerra°   thanklessly, wanders
65 quien todo el otro error de sí destierra.°[54]   exiles

Hágate temerosa
el caso de Anajérete,[55] y cobarde,°   subdued
que de ser desdeñosa
'se arrepintió° muy tarde;   she repented
70 y así su alma° con su mármol° arde.°[56]   soul, marble, burns

Estábase alegrando°   rejoicing

---

[51] The person referred to in "le" and "su" is the "cativo."

[52] The subject in these two verses is "dolor."

[53] The pronoun "él" refers to the "cativo."

[54] **No fuiste tú...** *You were not conceived or born of the hard earth. She who avoids all other errors should not be accused of thanklessly erring.* As with the Spanish "error," the English word "erring" means "wandering" as well as "making mistakes."

[55] In Greek mythology, the shepherd Iphis declared his love for the maiden Anaxarete, but was rejected. Anaxarete was still unmoved after Iphis killed himself in despair, so Aphrodite changed her to stone.

[56] **Hágate...** *May the case of Anaxarete make you fearful and subdued. She repented too late for being disdainful, and so her souls burns with her marble*

'del mal ajeno° el pecho° empedernido;°[57] of another's suffering, heart, ha
cuando abajo° mirando, downward
el cuerpo muerto vido° = vio
75 del miserable amante allí tendido;°[58] stretched out

Y al cuello el lazo° atado, noose
con que desenlazó° de la cadena° liberated, chain
el corazón cuitado;° aggrieved
que con su breve pena
80 compró la eterna punición° ajena.[59] punishment

Sintió allí convertirse
en piedad° amorosa el aspereza.°[60] pity, harshness
¡O tarde arrepentirse!° repentance
¡O última terneza!° tenderness
85 ¿Cómo te sucedió° mayor dureza? supplanted

Los ojos 'se enclavaron° became focused
en el tendido cuerpo que allí vieron;
los huesos 'se tornaron° became
más duros y crecieron,
90 y en sí° toda la carne° convirtieron.°[61] themselves, flesh, transformed

Las entrañas° heladas° bowels, ice-cold
tornaron poco a poco en piedra dura;
por las venas cuitadas

---

[57] The subject of the verb "[e]stábase alegrando" is "pecho."

[58] The subject of the verb "vido" is Anaxárete; the direct object is "cuerpo." In the next stanza, "lazo" is also a direct object of "vido."

[59] **Y al cuello...** And, tied to his neck, the noose with which he liberated his aggrieved heart from the chain. With his brief pain he bought the eternal punishment of someone else

[60] **Sintió...** She felt there the harshness change into loving pity.... At this point, Anaxarete begins her metamorphosis.

[61] **Los huesos...** The bones became harder and grew, and transformed all of the flesh into themselves

la sangre su figura
95 'iba desconociendo° y su natura;[62]   began to lose

Hasta que finalmente
en duro mármol vuelta y trasformada,
hizo de sí la gente
no tan maravillada,°   amazed
100 cuanto° de aquella ingratitud° vengada.°[63]   as, ingratitude, avenged

No quieras tú, señora,
de Némesis airada las saetas
probar, por Dios, agora;[64]
baste que tus perfetas
105 obras y hermosura a los poetas

Den° inmortal materia,[65]   provide
sin que también en verso lamentable
celebren la miseria
de algún caso° notable   incident
110 que por ti pase° triste y miserable.[66]   remains

---

[62] **Por las venas…** *In the aggrieved veins, the blood began to lose its form and nature*

[63] **Hasta que…** *Until at last, transformed into hard marble, she made people not so much amazed at her as avenged for that ingratitude of hers.*

[64] **No quieras tú…** *By God, Lady, do not now strive to test the arrows of angry Nemesis…* In Greek mythology, Nemesis was the goddess of divine justice and vengeance. Arrogance (*hubris*) was the chief target of her anger.

[65] **Baste que…** *Let it suffice for your perfect deeds and beauty to provide eternal material to the poets*

[66] The noun "poetas" from the previous stanza is the subject of "celebren."

Cristóbal de Castillejo (ca. 1490-1550)

CRISTÓBAL DE CASTILLEJO WAS born in Ciudad Rodrigo (near Salamanca, in northwest Spain) and spent his life in service to the Spanish crown after a brief stint in a Cistercian monastery in his youth. He was secretary to Charles V's brother Ferdinand, who later became king of Austria. He is most well known as the traditionalist opponent of the new "poesía italianizante" of Boscán and Garcilaso. He continued to write in the old style, though he was certainly capable of handling the new forms; one of his most famous works is a sonnet (one of the new, italianate forms) that criticizes the new style in general and Boscán and Garcilaso in particular. This sonnet is embedded in a longer poem, "Reprensión contra los poetas españoles que escriben en verso italiano." We have included the sonnet segment here. Opposition to this style often came from those who felt that native Spanish forms were superior to anything imported and were therefore perfectly adequate to portray a wide range of human experience. These traditional poetic forms also represented a link with what was perceived to be a more heroic past.

Later in life, Castillejo returned to the religious vocation of his youth. He was ordained and died in Vienna, where he had retired to a monastery.

Castillejo, Cristóbal de. *Obras*. Ed. J. Domínguez Bordona. 4 vols. Madrid: Clásicos Castellanos, 1926-1928.

SONETO

Garcilaso y Boscán[1], siendo llegados
al lugar donde están los trovadores[2]
que en esta nuestra lengua y sus primores°   beauty
fueron en este siglo señalados,°   famous

5   Los unos a los otros alterados°   agitated
se miran, 'con mudanza de colores °   growing pale
temiéndose que fuesen corredores°   scouts
espías o enemigos desmandados;°[3]   disobedient

Y juzgando primero por el traje,
10 pareciéronles ser, como debía,
gentiles° españoles caballeros;   elegant

---

[1] Garcilaso and Boscán, whose poems appear in this volume, imported the new poetic style from Italy. This poetry was referred to as "la poesía italianizante," or, roughly translated, "Italian-style Poetry." Two common forms of this new style of poetry were the sonnet and the lyre. Castillejo has written his critique of Garcilaso and Boscán in this imported sonnet form.

[2] **Siendo llegados...** *Having arrived at the place where the troubadours are.* The "place where the troubadors are" is Spain. Spain is here contrasted with Italy. Both Garcilaso and Boscán spent time in Italy: Garcilaso as a soldier, Boscán as a merchant. The word "troubadour" today generally refers loosely to minstrel-style singers. Originally, however, it referred to lyric poets who lived in Northern Spain, Southern France and Northern Italy in the eleventh through thirteenth centuries.

[3] **Los unos a los otros...** *The one group (of poets) looks at the other, agitated, growing pale, fearing that they [the other group of poets] were scouts, spies or disobedient enemies.* The last phrase "enemigos desmandados," has sometimes been translated "renegades," meaning traitors (to one's religion, country, political party or people.) The word "desmandado" comes from the verb "mandar," "to command." A "mandado" is a person who carries out someone's orders. A "desmandado" is someone who does not carry out orders and who has abandoned a commitment previously held; such a person seeks his own advantage.

Y oyéndoles hablar nuevo lenguaje[4]
mezclado de extranjera poesía,
con ojos los miraban de extranjeros.[5]

---

[4] "Nuevo lenguaje" refers to the new style of poetry imported from Italy.
[5] **Con ojos...** *They looked at them with the eyes of foreigners.*

Anónimo

SONETO

A Cristo Crucificado

    No me mueve°, mi Dios, para quererte   moves emotionally
el cielo que me tienes prometido;
ni me mueve el infierno tan temido
para dejar° por eso de ofenderte.[1]   to stop

5   Tú me mueves, Señor;° muéveme el verte   Lord
'clavado en° una cruz y escarnecido;°[2]   nailed to, mocked
muéveme ver tu cuerpo tan herido°;   wounded
muévenme tus afrentas° y tu muerte.[3]   insults

    Muéveme, en fin, tu amor, y en tal manera

---

[1] **No me mueve, mi Dios...** *The heaven you promised me does not move me to love you, my God; nor does the much-feared hell move me to stop offending you.* These lines refer to the theme of "disinterested" (i.e. "unselfish", *not* "uninterested") love towards God; that is, a devotional love towards the Creator unmotivated by either hope of reward or fear of punishment.

[2] **Muéveme el verte...** *It moves me to see you nailed to a cross and mocked.* The writer is addressing himself to Jesus Christ on the cross. In Christian theology, Christ is part of the Holy Trinity, or the triune God. This concept contains the idea that God the Father, God the Son (Jesus Christ) and God the Holy Spirit are three persons, one God. For this reason, the "mi Dios" addressed in the first quatrain is the same as Christ nailed to the cross in the second.

[3] **Muévenme tus afrentas...** *The insults you've suffered and your death move me*

10 que aunque no hubiera cielo, yo te amara,[4]
    y aunque no hubiera infierno, te temiera.[5]

    No tienes que me dar porque te quiera[6]
    pues aunque cuanto espero no esperara,[7]
    lo mismo que te quiero te quisiera.[8]

---

[4] **Aunque no hubiera cielo**... *Even if there were no heaven, I would still love you.* Note how here, as well as in the examples noted in footnotes 5 and 8, the imperfect subjunctive ("amara", "temiera", "quisiera") is used to convey the conditional ("would love", "would fear" and again "would love"). It is a common feature of the Spanish of this period to use the imperfect subjunctive instead of the conditional.

[5] **Aunque no hubiera infierno**... *Even if there were no hell I would still fear you*

[6] **No tienes que me dar**... *You don't have to give me a thing in order to make me love you*

[7] **Aunque cuanto**... *Even if I didn't hope what I do hope*

[8] **Lo mismo que**... *I would still love you the same as I do now*

Jorge de Montemayor (ca. 1520-1561)

JORGE DE MONTEMAYOR WAS the author of one of the bestselling books of the sixteenth-century. He was born in Portugal, of probably *converso* background, and spent most of his life in service to the Spanish crown as a soldier, courtier, musician, and singer. He served Philip II in Flanders and possibly traveled to England. Montemayor gained fame through his 1559 publication of *Los siete libros de la Diana*. We have included a fragment of it here as an example of the genre of pastoral poetry, although pastoral elements can be seen in other poems in this anthology. Pastoral literature ("la literatura pastoril"), prose or poetry that features shepherds suffering unrequited love in beautiful natural settings, was extremely popular in the sixteenth century, and it was inspired by the Bible and classical writers such as Theocritus and Virgil, as well as Petrarch and Boccaccio. A precursor of the *Diana* was the Italian Jacopo Sannazaro's *Arcadia* (Venice, 1502). The *Diana* is a story told in both prose and verse. Montemayor's work is an actual novel with a sustained plot line, centering around "el olvidado Sireno" who has been rejected by the Diana of the title. It also includes various other characters who have been unlucky in love. The selection presented here is the song of Arsileo, a shepherd in love.

Montemayor's *Diana* was reprinted in Spain many times, was soon translated into other European languages, and became as popular in other countries as it was in Spain. His work sparked many imitations both at home and abroad. Cervantes praised the quality of Montemayor's work and wrote his own pastoral novel, *La Galatea*. Shakespeare drew on the episode of Felix and Felismena for his *Two Gentlemen of Verona*. In addition to the *Diana*, Montemayor wrote both secular and religious poetry and several *autos sacramentales*.

Montemayor, Jorge de. *Los siete libros de la Diana*. Ed. Enrique Moreno Baez.

Madrid: Editorial Nacional, 1976.

Rhodes, Elizabeth. *The Unrecognized Precursors of Montemayor's Diana*. Columbia and London: U of Missouri P, 1992.

Solé-Leris, Amadeu. *The Spanish Pastoral Novel*. Boston: Twayne, 1980

GLOSA

Ven, ventura, ven y tura °

                     happiness, **dura** = stay

  ¡Qué tiempos, qué movimientos,
qué caminos tan extraños,
qué engaños, ° qué desengaños, °
qué grandes contentamientos °
5 nacieron de tantos daños! °

                     deceits, disillusions
                     contentments
                     harm

  Todo lo sufre una fe[1]
y un buen amor lo asegura, °
y 'pues que ° mi desventura °
ya denfadada ° se fue,
10 *ven, ventura, ven y tura.*

                     assures
                     since, unhappiness
                     = **desenfadada** *soothed*

  Sueles, ° ventura, moverte °
con ligero ° movimiento,
y si en darme este contento
no imaginas tener suerte,
15 más me vale mi tormento.

                     you tend, to move about
                     gentle

  Que si te vas, al partir
falta el seso ° y la cordura, °
mas si para estar segura
te determinas venir,
20 *ven, ventura, ven y tura.*

                     mind, good judgment

---

[1] **Todo lo sufre...** *Faith suffers from everything*

Si es en vano mi venida,
si acaso° vivo engañado,　　　　　　　　by chance
que todo teme un cuitado,°²　　　　　　　aggrieved person
¿no fuera perder la vida
25　consejo más acertado?°³　　　　　　　accurate

¡Oh temor, eres extraño!
Siempre el mal 'se te figura,°　　　　　　you imagine
mas ya que en tal hermosura
no puede caber engaño,
30　*ven, ventura, ven y tura.*

[de *Los siete libros de La Diana*]

---

² **Que todo teme...** *For an aggrieved person fears everything*
³ **¿No fuera...?** *Wouldn't more accurate advice lead to loss of life?*

Fray[1] Luis de León (1527-1591)

BORN IN BELMONTE, CUENCA (east of Madrid), of *converso* lineage, Fray Luis was one of the greatest minds of Renaissance Spain. The poems you will read in this anthology were not published during his lifetime, but were circulated privately. Francisco de Quevedo, whose poems also appear in this anthology, was the first editor and publisher of Fray Luis's poems. For Quevedo, Fray Luis was a model of clarity and elegance to be held up against what Quevedo felt were the excesses of the *culteranismo* movement.

Fray Luis was a theologian as well as a priest affiliated with a religious order (the Augustinians). He published his theological writings in Latin (which was the custom) but wrote other works for a wider audience in Spanish. He gained fame through *De los nombres de Cristo*, a philosophical meditation on different titles for Christ, and *La perfecta casada*, a manual for married women based on the description of the ideal wife described in the Old Testament, in Proverbs 31. In his drive to make the Bible more accessible, he translated the book of Job, the Song of Solomon, and other biblical texts into Spanish. Another of his great contributions to scholarship was his editing of the works of St. Teresa of Ávila.

Fray Luis's principal occupation was that of professor of theology at the University of Salamanca, with a specialty in Sacred Scripture. His academic specialty eventually led to his imprisonment. He was an outstanding linguist with an uncommon command of Hebrew; his unauthorized translation and distribution of the *Song of Solomon* got him into trouble with academic and ecclesiastical rivals, as did his insistence that the Latin translation of the Bible the Roman Catholic Church was using at the time (known as the Vulgate) contained numerous errors, and

---

[1] "Fray" corresponds to the word "friar" in English, and is generally used to refer to male members of certain religious orders.

that new, better translations from the original Hebrew and Greek were needed. His advocacy of a return to original sources provoked anxiety in the age of the Protestant Reformation, when arguments over how to interpret the Bible became dividing lines between ever-proliferating separatist religious movements. Having been reported to the Inquisition (anonymously) as teaching heretical propositions, Fray Luis spent over four years in prison (1572-1576) until he was cleared of the charges against him. His poem "A la salida de la cárcel" blames envy and lies for his imprisonment.

In *Poesía lírica del Siglo de Oro* Elias Rivers notes that Fray Luis's poetry typifies the way Spanish culture baptized or Christianized the Italian Renaissance (p. 345). One of the ways in which this is accomplished is in his incorporation of Christian Neo-Platonism into his work. This can be seen in Fray Luis's cosmology (vision of the universe) as hierarchically ordered with nature as copy or reflection of heavenly ideal forms. Christian Neo-Platonism was a strain of philosophical thought that reconciled Christianity with the teachings of Plato and Plotinus, and was thus a particularly appropriate vehicle for Catholic intellectuals such as Fray Luis to assimilate the best Classical pagan thought into their own creative work.

After Fray Luis was released from prison, he returned to his teaching position at the University of Salamanca. According to legend, his first words on returning to his classroom were, in Latin, "As we were saying yesterday..." Shortly before his death in 1591, he was elected Provincial of his order.

León, Luis de. *The Names of Christ*. Trans. Manuel Durán and William Kluback. New York: Paulist Press, 1984.

Macrí, Oreste. *La poesía de Fray Luis de León*. Salamanca: Anaya, 1970

ODA I

Vida retirada °

    withdrawn

    ¡Qué descansada° vida

    la° del que huye el mundanal° ruido,[2]

    y sigue la escondida

    senda,° por donde han ido

5 los pocos sabios° que en el mundo han sido;[3]

> restful
>
> = la *vida*, worldly
>
> path
>
> wise men

    Que no le enturbia° el pecho

    de los soberbios° grandes el estado,°[4]

    ni del dorado° techo

    'se admira,° fabricado°

10 del sabio moro,° en jaspe° sustentado!°[5]

> trouble
>
> proud, status
>
> gilded
>
> he marvels, created
>
> Moor, jasper columns, supported

    'No cura° si la fama

    canta con voz 'su nombre pregonera,°[6]

    ni cura si encarama°

    la lengua° lisonjera°

15 lo que condena la verdad sincera.[7]

> He doesn't care
>
> proclaiming his name
>
> praise
>
> tongue, flattering

    ¿Qué presta° a mi contento

    lends

---

[2] **¡Qué descansada...** *What a restful life, the life of the one who flees worldly noise*

[3] **Por donde...** *Where few wise men have gone*

[4] **Que no le enturbia...** *The status of the proud noblemen does not trouble his breast.* The "grandes" in Spain were grandees, society's most privileged aristocrats who claimed prestigious lineage and possessed most of society's wealth.

[5] **Ni del dorado...** *Nor does he marvel at the gilded ceiling, held up by jasper columns, made by the wise Moor!* This is a cultural reference to Moorish (North African Islamic) architecture, examples of which abound throughout Spain. It is a rich, ornate style. Jasper is a precious stone.

[6] **Con voz** ...*With loud voice proclaiming his name*

[7] **Ni cura...** *Nor does he care if flattering tongues praise that which sincere truth condemns*

si soy del vano dedo señalado,°8   pointed out
si, en busca deste viento,9
ando desalentado°   discouraged
20 con 'ansias vivas,° con mortal cuidado?°   intense anxiety, worries

   ¡Oh monte,° oh fuente,° oh río!   woodland, spring
   ¡Oh secreto seguro, deleitoso!°   delightful
   Roto casi el navío,°   ship
   a vuestro almo° reposo°   sacred, rest
25 huyo de aqueste mar tempestuoso.10

   Un no rompido sueño,
   un día puro, alegre, libre quiero;
   no quiero ver el ceño°   frown
   vanamente severo
30 'de a quien° la sangre ensalza° o el dinero.11   of the person whom, exalts

   'Despiértenme las aves°   birds
   con su cantar sabroso° 'no aprendido;°   delightful, unlearned
   no los 'cuidados graves°   grave concerns
   de que es siempre seguido°   followed

---

8 **¿Qué presta…** *What does it lend to my happiness if the vain finger points me out?*

9 The "wind" referred to is, in general, vanity—the things of this world which are not of permanent value. More specifically, the "wind" refers to the praise of superficial people referred to in the previous lines.

10 **Roto casi…** *The ship almost wrecked, to your sacred rest I flee from this stormy sea.* The "navío" refers to the speaker's soul. The adjective "almo" is a poetic term that can mean "sacred," "nourishing" or "venerable." The poet is addressing himself to the "monte…fuente…río" he called to at the beginning of the stanza.

11 **De a quien…** *Of the one who is exalted by blood line or money.* The ones exalted by lineage could be those of high societal rank or those who did not have Jewish ancestors.

35 el que al 'ajeno arbitrio° está atenido.°¹²

    the will of another, attendant on

   'Vivir quiero° conmigo,

    = quiero vivir,

gozar quiero del bien° que debo° al cielo,

    good things, I owe

'a solas,° sin testigo,°

    alone, witness

'libre de° amor, de celo,°

    free of, envy

40 de odio,° de esperanzas,° de recelo°.

    hatred, hopes, suspicion

   Del monte en la ladera,°

    hillside

por mi mano plantado tengo un huerto,°

    orchard

que con la primavera

de bella flor cubierto

45 ya muestra° en esperanza el fruto cierto.°¹³

    shows, sure

   Y 'como codiciosa°

    as if eager

por ver y acrecentar° su hermosura

    ,increase

desde° la cumbre° airosa°f

    rom, mountaintop, windy

una fontana° pura

    spring

50 hasta llegar corriendo 'se apresura.°¹⁴

    hastens

   Y luego, sosegada,°

    calm

el paso° entre los árboles torciendo,°¹⁵

    route, twisting

el suelo° 'de pasada°

    ground, in passing

de verdura° vistiendo°

    green, dressed

---

¹² **Despiértenme las aves…** *Let the birds wake me up with their lovely, unlearned singing, not the grave concerns that follow the man who is attendant on the will of another*

¹³ **Que con la primavera…** *That, with the arrival of spring, is covered with beautiful flowers, shows the hope of sure fruit.* This describes the orchard mentioned earlier in the stanza, the one planted by the poet.

¹⁴ **Y como codiciosa…** *And, as if eager to see and increase its beauty, a pure spring hastens from the windy mountaintop until it arrives rushing down*

¹⁵ **El paso…** *Making its way among the trees.* This still refers to the spring mentioned in the previous stanza.

55 y con diversas flores va esparciendo.[16]

El aire del huerto orea°   blows
y ofrece mil olores° al sentido;°   fragrances, the senses
los árboles menea°   sways
con un manso° ruido°   gentle, sound
60 que del oro y del cetro° pone olvido.°[17]   scepter, oblivion

---

[16] **El suelo...** *In passing, dressing the ground in green and scattering different flowers as it goes.* The subject of the sentence is still the "fontana" or spring of the previous stanza.

[17] **Los árboles menea...** *[The wind] sways the trees with a gentle noise that makes one forget gold and the scepter.*

ODA III

*A Francisco de Salinas, Catedrático ° de Música
de la Universidad de Salamanca*[18]   professor

El aire 'se serena °   becomes calm
y 'viste de° hermosura y luz 'no usada, °   dresses in, unusual
Salinas, cuando suena °   sounds
la música extremada, °   beautiful
5 por vuestra° sabia mano gobernada. °   your, directed

'A cuyo° son° divino   to whose, sound
el alma, ° que en olvido° está sumida, °   soul, forgetfulness, submerged
'torna a cobrar el tino°   recovers again its good sense
y memoria perdida
10 de su origen primera esclarecida. °[19]   illustrious

Y como 'se conoce, °   becomes aware of itself
en suerte y pensamientos 'se mejora; °   gets better
el oro desconoce, °   disregards
que el vulgo° vil° adora,   common people, despicable
15 la belleza caduca, ° engañadora. °[20]   fleeting, deceptive

Traspasa° el aire todo   Passes through
hasta llegar a la más alta esfera, °[21]   heavenly sphere

---

[18] Francisco Salinas was a professor of music, an organist, and a friend of Fray Luis. The University of Salamanca, founded in 1218 by King Alfonso of León, was one of the first universities established on the Iberian peninsula.

[19] The soul realizes the fact of its creation by God, God being the first illustrious origin. Note that the word "origen," usually masculine, is feminine here, hence the feminine adjectives "primera" and "esclarecida."

[20] **Y como se...** *And as [the soul] becomes aware of who it really is, it gets better in its luck and in its thoughts; it disregards what despicable, common people worship: gold; fleeting and deceptive beauty*

[21] **La más alta esfera...** *The highest region of the heavens.* During the Renaissance, it was widely believed that the planet Earth was surrounded by

y oye allí 'otro modo°   another kind
de 'no perecedera°   undying
20 música, que es de todas la primera.[22]

    Ve cómo 'el gran maestro,°   God
aquesta° inmensa cítara° aplicado,[23]   esta, cithara
con movimiento diestro°   skillful
produce el son° sagrado°   melody, sacred
25 con que este eterno templo es sustentado.

    Y como está compuesta°   made up
de números concordes,° luego envía°   concordant, sends
consonante° respuesta;°   harmonious, answer
y 'entrambas a porfía°   both competing
30 se mezcla una dulcísima armonía.[24]

---

multiple, concentric bands known as spheres. This belief, supported by the writings of ancient thinkers such as Pythagoras, Aristotle, and Ptolemy, held that as these spheres revolved around the Earth they moved the heavenly bodies (the moon, the sun, the known planets, the stars) that could be seen with the naked eye. It was thought that the spheres, and thus the heavenly bodies, moved according to mathematical laws of harmony and proportion. It was also believed that the harmonious and proportional contact that each moving sphere had with each adjacent, moving sphere could be perceived and reflected on Earth in the intervals of plucked strings on citharas, lyres, harps, and other instruments. In Renaissance cosmology, the highest region of the heavens (beyond the outermost moving sphere) was the Empyrean, the domain of God.

[22] It is important to realize that the motion of the soul is upwards, passing from the center and lowest point, Earth, through all of the spheres (hence the "todo"), finally arriving at the highest regions. The "undying music" is the First Music, the source of all other music.

[23] **Ve cómo ...** *It* [the soul] *sees how the great Maestro* [God], *dedicated to the playing of the great cithara.* The cithara was a stringed instrument used by the ancient Greek poets. Other possible translations of "cítara" are zither, lyre, or harp.

[24] **Y como...** *And as it* [the soul] *is made up of concordant numbers, it then sends a harmonious answer; and both, competing, produce a very sweet harmony.* Here, the adjective "compuesta" is modifying "alma", which appeared several stanzas ago,

Aquí la alma navega°   navigates
por un mar de dulzura,° y finalmente   sweetness
en él ansí° 'se anega°   **así**, it sinks
que ningún accidente
35 extraño y peregrino° oye o siente.°25   foreign, perceives

¡Oh, desmayo° dichoso!°   swoon, blissful
¡Oh, muerte que das vida! ¡Oh, dulce olvido!
¡Durase° en tu reposo,°   If only I could remain, tranquilit[y]
sin ser restituido°   brought back
40 jamás° a aqueste bajo y vil sentido!°26   ever, realm of the senses

A este bien° os llamo,27   good [thing]
gloria del apolíneo° sacro° coro,°   divine, sacred, chorus
amigos a quien° amo   = **quienes**
'sobre todo tesoro;°   above all treasure

in line 7. "Concordant" means "in agreement." Elias Rivers (*Renaissance and Baroque Poetry*, 95) translates the phrase "números concordes" as "harmonizing elements." Fray Luis here refers to the idea of the "music of the spheres." The mention of numbers connects the musical themes of the poem to the ideas of the ancient Greek mathematician Pythagoras, who observed and measured numerical relationships between musical tones and pitches. According to Pythagoras, all existing phenomena, including the human soul, have an underlying mathematical reality.

25 **En él ansí...** *So sinks in it that it neither hears nor perceives any strange or foreign discordant notes..* "Se anega" could also translate as "drowns." The word "accidente" is a musical term referring to sharp or flat notes. Though this term would not necessarily translate as "discordant notes" in other contexts, we think this particular translation does express Fray Luis' meaning; however, it is not necessarily limited to that meaning.

26 **Sin ser...** *Without ever being brought back to this low and despicable realm of the senses!* The blissful swoon, life-giving death and sweet oblivion all describe the state of the soul in union with God. Everything in this earthly life, by comparison, is "bajo y vil."

27 The "os" will be clarified in the following lines: Fray Luis is calling to his friends, specifically poets and musicians.

45 que 'todo lo visible° es triste lloro.° [28]   *everything that can be seen, weeping*

    ¡Oh, suene 'de contino,°[29]   **de continuo** = *for all eternity*
    Salinas, vuestro son en mis oídos,°   *ears*
    por quien al 'bien divino°   *divine good*
    despiertan los sentidos
50 quedando° a 'lo demás° amortecidos!°[30]   *remaining, everything else, deadened*

---

[28] Apollo was the god of music and poetry. The phrase "todo lo visible" refers to this earthly life, in contrast to the heavenly one, By comparison, this life is sad tears. Also, in *Five Centuries of Spanish Literature*, Linton Barrett notes that "todo lo visible" alludes to the fact that Salinas was blind (150n).

[29] **Suene de contino...**Let it [the music] sound continuously, more poetically, for all eternity.

[30] **Por quien al...** By which the senses awaken to divine goodness, remaining deadened to everything else. The phrase "por quien" refers to "vuestro son" in the previous line.

ODA VIII

Noche Serena

Cuando contemplo el cielo[31]
de innumerables° luces adornado, countless
y miro hacia° el suelo° towards, earth
de noche rodeado,° surrounded
5　en sueño y en olvido sepultado,°[32] wrapped

El amor y la pena° grief
despiertan en mi pecho° un ansia° ardiente;° breast, desire, burning
despiden° larga vena° release, flood
los ojos hechos fuente;[33]
10　'La lengua° dice al fin con voz doliente:° my tongue, sorrowful

«Morada° de grandeza,° dwelling place, grandeur
templo de claridad y hermosura,
el alma,° que a tu alteza° soul, height
nació, ¿qué desventura° misery
15　la tiene en esta cárcel baja, escura?°[34] oscura

---

[31] Spanish does not make a distinction between "sky" and "heaven." Both senses of "cielo" should be kept in mind here.

[32] **De noche...** *Surrounded by night, wrapped in sleep and forgetfulness.* In this stanza, "adornado" modifies "cielo"; "rodeado" and "sepultado" modify "suelo." Also, "sepultado" literally means buried; figuratively, it means hidden or wrapped. Forgetfulness or oblivion in Fray Luis's poetry refers to the Christian Neoplatonic idea of the soul failing to realize its origin in God.

[33] **Despiden larga...** *My eyes, having become a fountain, release a flood of tears.* The subject of the verb "despiden" is "los ojos." Our translation of "flood" for "vena" is more figurative than literal.

[34] The "la" is merely duplicating the direct object "desventura" for emphasis and metrical considerations and should not be translated. The "cárcel baja, escura" (*low, dark prison*) is the body, which in Platonic thought is the prison of the soul.

¿Qué mortal° desatino°   deadly, folly
de la verdad aleja° así 'el sentido,°³⁵   alienates, my senses
que, de tu 'bien divino°   divine good
olvidado,° perdido   forgetting
20 sigue la vana° sombra, el 'bien fingido?°³⁶   vain, false good

     El hombre está entregado°   given over
al sueño, de su suerte° 'no cuidando;°   fate, careless
y, con paso° callado,°   progress, silent
el cielo, 'vueltas dando,°   revolving
25 las horas del vivir 'le va hurtando.°³⁷   steals from him

     ¡Oh, despertad,° mortales!°   awaken, mortal men
Mirad con atención en vuestro° daño.°³⁸   your, damage
Las almas inmortales,
'hechas a bien tamaño,°   made for such great things
30 ¿podrán vivir de sombra y de engaño?°   deception

     ¡Ay, levantad los ojos
aquesta° celestial° eterna esfera!°³⁹   **esta**, heavenly, sphere

---

³⁵ **De la verdad...** *Alienates my senses from the truth.* In this stanza, "el sentido" is the English "senses." Moreover, the poet is referring to his own senses, though he does not use the possessive adjective "mi" to modify "sentido." Unlike English, Spanish language conventions tend to resist constant assertions of personal possession.

³⁶ It is the senses (in Spanish, the singular "sentido") that are forgetful (of their divine origin), lost and following after vain shadows and false ideas of what is good.

³⁷ "El cielo" is the subject of the present progressive verb "va hurtando," which we have translated into the simple present tense; it is modified by the phrase "con paso callado."

³⁸ **Mirad con...** *Look with close attention to the things that do your soul damage*

³⁹ In the Renaissance, it was believed that the Earth was surrounded by several concentric spheres. As these spheres revolved, they moved the heavenly bodies (the moon, the sun, the known planets, the stars) that could be seen with the naked eye. The outermost and final sphere, the Empyrean, was believed to

burlaréis° los antojos°   you will mock, fickleness
de aquesa° 'lisonjera   esa
35 vida,° con cuanto° teme° y cuanto espera.[40]   life of flattery, all that, it fears

¿Es más que un breve° punto°   tiny, point
el bajo y torpe° suelo,° comparado   crude, Earth
a aqueste gran trasunto,°[41]   Representation
do vive mejorado°   in a better way
40 lo que es, lo que será, lo que ha pasado?

Quien mira el gran concierto
de aquestos° resplandores° eternales,   estos, radiances
su movimiento cierto°   sure
sus pasos° desiguales°   steps, unequal
45 y en proporción° concorde° tan iguales;[42]   proportion, harmonious

La luna cómo mueve

---

be the domain of God. The "celestial eterna esfera" here thus refers to God's eternal domain.

[40] **Con cuanto...** *With all it fears and hopes for.* The "it" is the "lisonjera vida" of the previous lines.

[41] **Es más que...** *Is the crude and lowly earth anything more than a tiny point in comparison with this great Representation?* Ancient and medieval thinkers conceived of the earth as an insignificant "point" in comparison with the great spaces of the universe. We have translated "trasunto" as "Representation." It can also be translated as "copy" or "imitation." This is a philosophical and theological term. The cosmos is a copy of God. It is also a theophany, or, manifestation of God. The lower you are, the cruder the quality of this copy. The higher you go, the more faithful the copy is in representing God, and the more it shares in God's actual being. This is why we used a capital "R," to convey the higher sphere's greater sharing in the nature of the divine Being.

[42] The eternal radiances (the planets) are about to be described in the stanzas that follow. Their movements are described as a concert (the music of the spheres), and are at the same time sure or fixed, in that they follow a constant path, unequal in their steps in that every celestial body travels a different distance, each being closer to or farther from the center point, Earth. Yet they are harmoniously proportionate to each other in their complementary differences.

la plateada° rueda, y va 'en pos della°   silver, behind her
la luz do el saber° llueve,°   knowledge, rains down
y la graciosa° estrella   graceful
50 de amor la sigue reluciente° y bella;[43]   shining bright

Y cómo otro camino
prosigue° el sanguinoso° Marte airado, [44]   follows, bloody
y el Júpiter benino,°[45]   **benigno** = kindly
'de bienes mil cercado,°   surrounded by much goodness
55 serena° el cielo con su rayo° amado;°   calms, rays, beloved

Rodéase° en la cumbre°   revolves, summit
Saturno, padre de los 'siglos de oro;°   golden age
tras° él la muchedumbre°   after, multitude
del reluciente coro°   chorus of stars
60 'su luz va repartiendo y su tesoro:°[46]   shares their light and treasure

¿Quién es el que esto mira
y precia° la bajeza° de la tierra,[47]   values, lowliness
y no gime° y suspira°   moan, sigh
y rompe 'lo que encierra°   what locks
65 el alma y 'destos bienes la destierra?°   exiles it from this good

---

[43] This stanza begins a survey of the spheres. Fray Luis refers to the moon as a silver wheel here; the spheres were sometimes called wheels. The light where knowledge rains down is Mercury (messenger of the gods) and the graceful planet of love is Venus (goddess of love).

[44] In classical mythology, Mars is the god of war.

[45] In classical mythology, Jupiter is the chief of the gods.

[46] Saturn, god of agriculture and father of Jupiter in classical mythology, reigned over a golden age of equality and peace. He is at the summit, or highest point, of the planetary spheres. After that, there is the sphere of the stars, which in this stanza is the "reluciente coro." They are described in musical terms just as the movement of all the celestial bodies is described in line 41 as a "concierto." Again, the movement of the spheres in the heavens is conceived of as a musical dance.

[47] **Quién es él...** *Who can see this and value the lowly earth?*

Aquí vive el contento,°   happiness
aquí reina° la paz; aquí, asentado°   reigns, seated
en rico y alto asiento,°   seat
está el 'Amor sagrado,°   God
70 'de glorias y deleites rodeado.°   surrounded by glories and deli

Inmensa hermosura
aquí 'se muestra° toda,[48] y resplandece°   is shown, shines
clarísima° luz pura,   the brightest
que jamás° anochece;°   never, turns to darkness
75 eterna primavera aquí florece.°   blooms

¡Oh campos verdaderos!°[49]   true
¡Oh prados° con verdad frescos° y amenos!°   meadows, cool, pleasant
¡Riquísimos mineros!°   mines
¡Oh deleitosos° senos!°   delightful, refuges
80 ¡Repuestos° valles, de mil bienes° llenos!»   hidden, blessings

---

[48] **Inmensa hermosura...** *Here immense beauty is shown in its fullness*
[49] The fields are described as "true." This means that the poet is contemplating those true fields in heaven, of which earthly fields are only a copy or a muddy reflection.

ODA XXIII

A la salida ° de la cárcel[50]   exit

   Aquí la envidia° y mentira   envy
me tuvieron encerrado.°   imprisoned
Dichoso° el humilde° estado°   happy, humble, condition
del sabio° que 'se retira°   wise man, withdraws
5 de aqueste° mundo malvado,°   **este**, wicked

   y con pobre° mesa y casa   modest
en el campo deleitoso°   delightful
con sólo Dios 'se compasa°[51]   paces oneself
y 'a solas° su vida pasa   alone
10 ni envidiado° ni envidioso.°   envied, envious

[50] "On Leaving Prison." Fray Luis was imprisoned for almost five years.
[51] **Con sólo...** *Lives at God's pace alone*

Santa Teresa de Ávila (1515-1582)

SAINT TERESA WAS BOTH a nun who reformed a religious order as well as a mystic who wrote of her personal spiritual experiences of divine phenomena. She is also one of the most well-known Spaniards of all time. Her fame is due to her having been proclaimed both Saint and Doctor of the Roman Catholic Church. It is due as well to her writings, which have been published and translated continuously since her death. Teresa produced spiritual autobiography, historical accounts of her foundations of convents, books of spiritual counsel, letters, songs, and poems, among other things. Her prolific documentation of her own life and, by extension, of her time, provides us with valuable insight into the daily life of women in sixteenth-century Spain. These types of documents enrich our knowledge of the private sphere that women inhabited, a sphere often overlooked in other forms of writing.

Teresa is known by several names, owing to both her historical status as a saint of the Roman Catholic Church and her social status within sixteenth-century Castilian society. She is known generally in English by the city of her birth: Saint Teresa of Ávila. In Spanish, she may be referred to merely as Santa Teresa, Santa Teresa de Ávila or as Santa Teresa de Jesús, the "de Jesús" being the name she chose for herself on her profession as a nun. Her secular name was Teresa de Cepeda y Ahumada. On her father's side, she was a descendant of *conversos*, Jewish converts to Christianity.

Teresa was born in Ávila in 1515, entered the Carmelite convent of the Incarnation in 1535 and was professed a nun there in 1537. During her life as a professed religious (member of a religious order, in this case, the Carmelites), Teresa underwent what she believed to be important spiritual experiences in the form of direct contact with God; eventually, she came to believe that God was calling her to reform the Carmelites and return the order to its original, rigorous purity. Such reform would involve the imposition of a new, harder rule on members and many of those connected to her interpreted her proposals as exercises in narcissism, self-righteousness, and self-deception. Her ecclesiastical superiors investigated her experiences and ordered her to write about them, the better to scrutinize them for heresy. Eventually, Teresa was cleared and her reforms went forward, though not without a great degree of opposition and hardship. She died in 1582 and was canonized a saint by Pope Gregory XV in 1622. Her standing within the Catholic Church was further enhanced when Pope Paul VI declared her a Doctor of the Church in 1970. This new status meant that her spiritual writings not only conformed to Church teaching but indeed represented it; as such, these teachings carry a great deal of authority and should be taken seriously by the faithful.

While Teresa is not usually considered a major poet, her verse contains its own delights and holds historical and spiritual interest for the modern reader. These poems express Teresa's own experience of God and do so in a different way from her prose narrative, which is more detailed and, paradoxically, harder to grasp in its totality. The poems were often occasional, that is, written for special occasions (holidays, saints' feast days, etc). Teresa wrote for the diversion, recreation, and spiritual edification of the nuns in her convents and, in so doing, reveals to us not only her character but also the type of spirituality flourishing under her guidance and direction. As a towering figure of world spirituality, Teresa as poet deserves such interest.

Efrén de la Madre de Dios y Otger Steggink, ed. and trans. *Obras completas.* By Santa Teresa de Jesús. Madrid: La Editorial Católica, 1974.

Kavanaugh, Kieran and Otilio Rodríguez. *The Collected Works of St. Teresa of Ávila.* 3 vols. Washington, D.C.: ICS Publications, 1976–85.

Medwick, Cathleen. *Teresa of Ávila: The Progress of a Soul.* New York: Doubleday, 1999.

Muero porque no muero[1]

    Vivo sin vivir en mí[2]
y tan 'alta vida° espero   heaven
Que muero porque no muero.

    Vivo ya fuera° de mí,   outside
5 'Después que° muero de amor,   since
Porque vivo en el Señor,°   Lord
Que me quiso para sí;°[3]   himself
Cuando el corazón le di
Puso en él este letrero:°[4]   sign
10 *Que muero porque no muero.*

    Esta divina prisión,
Del amor con que yo vivo,
Ha hecho a mi Dios mi cautivo°   captive
Y libre mi corazón;
15 Y causa en mí tal pasión

---

[1] **Muero porque no...** *I die because I am not dying.* The title of the poem, which appears as a refrain several times within the body of the poem, is a paradox: the speaker feels as if she is dying (experiencing a deep suffering and, simultaneously, desire) because she is not actually physically dying, or going to be in the presence of Christ, who is the true Life.

[2] **Vivo sin vivir...** *I live without living in myself.* This is a logical extension of the paradox of the refrain. Living in the presence of Christ is so joyous that being in this earthly life is not truly living. The mystic experiences ecstasy; the word "ecstasy" is from the Greek *ekstasis*, which means, being outside of one's place, or by extension, being outside of oneself. True life is gained, paradoxically, by forsaking the pursuit of this false earthly life.

[3] **Que me quiso...** *Who wanted me for himself.* The relationship between God and the soul is analogous to that of a male lover (God) and a female beloved (the soul). The word "alma" is feminine in Spanish, and in the Christian mystical tradition, the soul plays a feminine role in relationhip to the masculine God.

[4] **Puso en él...** *He (God) put on it (Teresa's heart) this sign.* The sign on the speaker's heart repeats the refrain, "que muero porque no muero."

Ver a mi Dios prisionero,[5]
Que muero porque no muero.

¡Ay, qué larga es esta vida!
¡Qué duros° estos destierros,° tough, exiles
20 Esta cárcel y estos hierros° shackles
En que el alma° está metida!°[6] soul, placed
Sólo esperar la salida° death
Me causa dolor tan fiero,° fierce
Que muero porque no muero.

25 ¡Ay, qué vida tan amarga° bitter
Do° no 'se goza° el Señor! **donde**, is enjoyed
Porque si es dulce el amor,
No lo es la esperanza° larga:[7] hope
Quíteme Dios[8] esta carga° load
30 Más pesada° que el acero,° heavy, steel
Que muero porque no muero.

Sólo con la confianza° confidence
Vivo de que 'he de morir,° I am to die
Porque muriendo 'el vivir° life
35 Me asegura° mi esperanza.[9] assures
Muerte do el vivir 'se alcanza,° is reached

---

[5] Verses 11-14 speak of God as captive in a divine prison of love, i.e., the heart which the poet gave to him. This divine prison has paradoxically made God a captive and the poetic speaker (i.e., Teresa), a captive of this life, free. It is a playful rendering of the relationship between God and the soul. Intimacy with God is a theme of much of Teresa's writing.

[6] Verses 19-21 use exile, prison, and shackles to describe this earthly life; the soul is the prisoner of the body.

[7] **Qué vida tan...** *What a bitter life, in which the Lord is not [cannot be] enjoyed!. For if love is sweet, the long wait isn't.* The "lo" echoes the "dulce" of the previous phrase. This is known as the "resumptive lo."

[8] **Quíteme Dios...** *May God take away from me*

[9] **Me asegura...** *My hope is assured.*

'No te tardes,° que te espero,[10]   Don't delay
Que muero porque no muero.

    Mira que el amor es fuerte;
40 Vida, no me seas molesta,°   troublesome
    Mira que sólo 'te resta,°   remains to you
    Para ganarte,° perderte;[11]   gain yourself
    Venga ya la dulce muerte,
    Venga 'el morir° muy ligero,°   death, swiftly
45 *Que muero porque no muero.*

    Aquella vida 'de arriba,°   from heaven
    Que es la vida verdadera,
    Hasta que esta vida muera
    No se goza estando viva.
50 Muerte, no seas esquiva;°   unfriendly
    Viva muriendo primero,[12]
    Que muero porque no muero.

    Vida, ¿qué puedo yo darle
    A mi Dios que vive en mí,
55 Si no es perderte a ti
    Para mejor a Él gozarle?[13]
    Quiero muriendo alcanzarle,
    Pues a Él solo es al que quiero,[14]
    Que muero porque no muero.

---

[10] **Muerte, do el...** *Death, which touches life, don't be late, I'm waiting for you*

[11] **Vida, no me...** *Life, trouble me not. See that the only thing that remains for you to gain yourself, is to lose yourself.* This echoes Christ's words, "For whosoever will save his life shall lose it: and whosoever will lose his life for my sake shall find it." (Matthew 16:25).

[12] **Viva, muriendo...** *Let me live by first dying*

[13] **Vida, ¿qué puedo...** Life, what can I give to my God who lives in me, but the losing of you in order to better enjoy Him?

[14] **Quiero muriendo...** *I want to reach Him by dying, since He is the only one I love*

Nada te turbe°[15]   upset

    Nada te turbe,
    Nada te espante,°[16]   disturb
    Todo 'se pasa,°   passes away
    Dios no 'se muda,°   changes
5 La paciencia
    'Todo lo alcanza;°   obtains everything
    Quien a Dios tiene
    Nada 'le falta.°   lacks
    Sólo Dios 'basta.°   is enough

---

[15] This poem is widely known among devout Catholics as "St. Teresa's Bookmark." It was found in Teresa's breviary (prayer book) after her death. It was translated into English by the American poet and professor of Modern Languages Henry Wadsworth Longfellow and has been reprinted many times on prayer cards and in other devotional materials.

[16] **Nada te turbe...** *Let nothing upset you, let nothing frighten you.* Both the verbs "turbar" (to upset or disturb) and "espantar" (to scare or frighten) are in the subjunctive in a way that sometimes confuses an English speaker, as they appear in main clauses. Very often, intermediate to advanced levels of language instruction emphasize the function of the subjunctive in subordinate clauses to such an extent that students beginning the study of literature may not always know what to do with the subjunctive when it appears outside of that context. When, as in this case, the subject of a verb is in the third person ("nada"), we can translate it as "let" or "may" + subject + verb.

Mi Amado °es para mí — Beloved (i.e., Christ)

    Ya 'toda me entregué° y di[17], — *I surrendered myself entirely*
y 'de tal suerte° he trocado,° — *in such a way, changed*
que mi Amado es para mí
y yo soy para mi Amado.[18]

5   Cuando el dulce Cazador° [19] — Hunter (i.e., God)
me tiró° y dejó° herida,° [20] — shot (with an arrow), left, woun
en los brazos del amor
mi alma° 'quedó rendida,° — soul, was surrendered
y 'cobrando nueva vida° — getting new life back
10 'de tal manera° he trocado, — in such a way
que mi Amado es para mí
y yo soy para mi Amado.

    Hirióme° con una flecha° — He wounded me, arrow
enherbolada° de amor, — poisoned with herbs
15 y mi alma 'quedó hecha° — was made

---

[17] **Ya toda me...** *I surrendered and gave myself entirely.* Teresa is referring to spiritual union with God, often compared to a romantic relationship between lovers. Other versions of the poem have "yo" instead of "ya" as the first word. The "ya" can be seen an intensifier of the sentiment.

[18] **Que mi Amado...** This is a quotation from the Bible, specifically the Song of Solomon 2:16: "My beloved is mine, and I am his...." Teresa uses the Song of Solomon much the same way that John of the Cross does: the two lovers in the erotic poem are an analogy of the relationship between the soul and God.

[19] God as a "sweet Hunter" is a paradox in which the prey is hunted in order to be transformed and resurrected. This figure of a sweet Hunter is also a sacred parody of the pagan figure of Cupid, Roman god of love, whose arrows cause those wounded by them to fall hopelessly in love.

[20] For an explanation of the idea of God "wounding" the soul with love, see the notes for the poetry of John of the Cross, specifically the note to line 2 in "Canción III: Llama de amor viva," the note to line 4 in "Cántico espiritual," and the note to line 34 in "Noche oscura."

una con su Criador;°[21]   Creator

'ya yo no quiero° otro amor,   I no longer want

pues a mi Dios me he entregado,

y mi Amado es para mí

20   *y yo soy para mi Amado.*

---

[21] **Mi alma quedó...** My soul was made one with her Creator.

San Juan de la Cruz (1542-1591)

SAN JUAN DE LA Cruz, known in English as Saint John of the Cross, was born Juan de Yepes in Fontiveros, a small town between Madrid and Salamanca. Like Saint Teresa of Ávila, he was made a saint and Doctor of the Roman Catholic Church. Also like Saint Teresa, he is considered a great spiritual teacher. He is considered a major poet not just in Spain but in world literature. Within the Roman Catholic Church, he is a powerful theologian who deeply influenced the late Pope John Paul II, who wrote his doctoral dissertation on the writings of this great Spaniard.

Juan de Yepes was born into crushing poverty in 1542. The reason for this poverty was that his father, Gonzalo de Yepes, had been disowned by his family. In marrying Juan's mother, Catalina Álvarez (a woman of more humble background than the silk-merchant Yepes family), Gonzalo gave up an inheritance and a comfortable lifestyle to become a poor weaver like his wife. When Juan was still a child, his father died, as did one of his brothers. Juan's mother moved the family, now destitute, to Medina del Campo (north of Salamanca) where there were more opportunities for work.

Juan's excellent performance as a pupil in his school, as an altar-server in church, and later as a nurse in a local hospital led to his being noticed and encouraged to further his education. He entered the Jesuit school where he was introduced to a classical education, the influence of which can be discerned in his learned poetry. In 1563 he entered the Carmelite religious order and soon after arrived at the University of Salamanca to begin studies in Philosophy and Theology. Fray Luis de León was a professor of theology there at this time, though it is not known if the two ever crossed paths. In 1567, while still a student at the university, Juan was ordained a priest in Salamanca; later that same year, he met St. Teresa, who told him of her desire to reform the Carmelite order and return it to its original, or primitive, observance. Juan joined himself to Teresa's efforts and zealously pursued the reform of the male branch of the Carmelites.

Juan's efforts, like Teresa's, provoked severe tensions within the order and he was arrested by certain Carmelites and other concerned parties, and held in a monastery prison in Toledo for nine months in terrible conditions. Near death, he managed to escape from this prison in August 1578. It is generally believed that he wrote his poems during this incarceration.

Juan went on to perform various duties, administrative and otherwise, within the order. His last years were marked by travels and new foundations of Discalced, or, reformed Carmelite monasteries. He died in 1591 in Úbeda, a town in Andalusia. He was canonized a saint of the Roman Catholic Church in 1726 by Pope Benedict XIII and was declared a Doctor of the church in 1926 by Pope Pius XI.

Alonso, Dámaso. *La poesía de San Juan de la Cruz (desde esta ladera)*. Madrid: M. Aguilar, 1946.

San Juan de la Cruz. *The Collected Works of St. John of the Cross*. Trans. Kieran Kavanaugh and Otilio Rodríguez. Washington, DC: ICS Publications, 1991.

Wojtila, Karol (Pope John Paul II). *Gift and Mystery: On the Fiftieth Anniversary of my Priestly Ordination*. New York: Doubleday, 1996

CANCIÓN I

Cántico espiritual[1]

Canciones entre el alma ° y el esposo   soul

Esposa:
  ¿Adónde 'te escondiste,°   did you hide
  amado, y me dejaste 'con gemido?°   moaning
  Como el ciervo° huiste,°[2]   stag, you fled
  'habiéndome herido;°[3]   having wounded me
5 salí° tras° ti, clamando,° y eras ido.°   I went, after, crying out, gone

---

[1] The word "cántico" translates directly as "canticle" or "song." An alternate title of the *Song of Solomon* is the "Canticle of Canticles" or simply as the "Canticle." John's poem is a rewriting of the *Song of Solomon*, a book of the Hebrew Scriptures or Old Testament, as it is read in the Christian tradition. Like the biblical document, it has a dramatic dialogue, which takes place between the *alma* or *esposa* (the bride, who is the human soul) and the *esposo* (the bridegroom, who is Christ.) Also, there is a chorus of *Criaturas* or, all of nature. In it, as in the "Noche oscura," the soul, portrayed as a woman, becomes aware of the absence of the lover (Christ) and therefore is filled with desire for Him, and goes out in search of Him. John wrote commentaries on his poems, and we will be using these commentaries to explain some of the more difficult passages. These commentaries can be found gathered in one volume in *The Collected Works of St. John of the Cross*, translated and edited by Kieran Kavanaugh and Otilio Rodríguez (Washington, D.C.: ICS Publications, 1991), hereafter referred to as "Kavanaugh/Rodríguez," followed by the page number on which John's commentary appears.

[2] **Como el ciervo...** *You fled like the stag.* Here the bridegroom is compared by the bride to a stag because of the speed with which he appears and disappears, similar to the visitation of Christ in the soul.

[3] The "wounds" of love are ways in which the soul is touched during Christ's visitation. In his commentary, St. John describes them as fiery arrows that leave the soul passionately aflame with love (Kavanaugh/Rodríguez, 484).

Pastores,° los que fuerdes°⁴
allá, por las majadas,° al otero,°
si 'por ventura° vierdes°⁵
'aquél que° yo más° quiero,
10 decidle° que adolezco,° peno° y muero.

    Shepherds, go
    sheepfolds, knoll
    by chance, you see
    that one whom, the most
    tell him, I'm ill, I suffer

Buscando mis amores,°
iré por esos montes° y riberas;°
ni cogeré° las flores,
ni temeré° las fieras,°
15 y pasaré los fuertes° y fronteras.°⁶

    love
    woodlands, riversides
    will pick
    I will fear, wild beasts
    strong men, frontiers

Pregunta a las Criaturas:
    ¡Oh bosques° y espesuras,°
plantadas por la mano del amado!
¡Oh 'prado de verduras,°
de flores esmaltado,°
20 decid 'si por vosotros ha pasado!°

    woods, thickets

    green meadow
    adorned
    if he has passed your way

Respuesta° de las Criaturas:
    Mil gracias° derramando,°
pasó por estos sotos° con presura,°
y yéndolos° mirando,
con sola su figura°
25 vestidos° los dejó de hermosura.⁷

    answer
    graces, pouring out
    groves, haste
    passing by them
    face
    clothed

---

⁴ **Pastores, los que...** *Shepherds, you who go.* The verb "fuerdes" is a rusticated, or peasant-style way of saying "fuereis," which is the future subjunctive (now mostly obsolete) of "ir" with "vos" as its subject. In his commentary, St. John says the shepherds are the soul's desires (Kavanaugh/Rodríguez, 484). In general, the future subjunctive can be translated by the simple present tense in English.

⁵ Like "fuerdes" in the previous note, "vierdes" is a rusticated form of "viereis," the future subjunctive of "ver" with "vos" as its subject.

⁶ The enemies of the soul (Kavanaugh/Rodríguez, 492).

⁷ **Yéndolos mirando...** *As he passed them by, looking, with only (the sight of) his face, he left them [the "sotos," or groves] clothed with beauty*

Esposa:

¡Ay, quién podrá sanarme!°   heal me
'Acaba de entregarte° ya 'de vero;°   give yourself over, **de veras**
'no quieras enviarme°   don't try to send me
'de hoy° 'más ya mensajero,°   from today on, any more messe[?]
30   que no saben decirme lo que quiero.

Y todos cuantos vagan,°⁸   wander freely
de ti me van mil gracias refiriendo.°⁹   telling
Y todos más 'me llagan,°   wound me
y déjame° muriendo   = me deja
35   un no sé qué que quedan balbuciendo.°¹⁰   stammering

Mas ¿cómo perseveras,
oh vida, no viviendo donde vives,¹¹
y haciendo, porque mueras,
las flechas° que recibes,   arrows

----

⁸ **Y todos cuantos vagan...** *And all those who wander freely.* In his commentary, St. John says that this passage refers to rational beings, i.e., humans and angels (Kavanaugh/Rodríguez, 499-500).

⁹ **De ti me...** *Tell me of your many graces.* The subject of the verb "van...refiriendo" is "todos cuantos vagan."

¹⁰ **Y déjame muriendo...** *And an I-don't-know-what that they keep murmuring leaves me dying.* Our translation of "un no sé que" is literal and crude. Rivers captures it well with "something mysterious." (*Renaissance and Baroque Poetry of Spain*, 132) In any case, the mysterious something would be those sublime realities of God that the soul does not yet know. According to St. John in his commentary, these are "stammered" by those who wander freely, that is, rational beings, meaning angels and humans, whose articulations of the experience of God fall grossly short of expressing the reality of it, no matter how hard they try (Kavanaugh/Rodríguez, 502).

¹¹ **No viviendo donde...** *Not living where you live.* A typical paradox of mystical and devotional writing, in that the true home of the soul is with Christ, not in the body.

40 de lo que del amado en ti concibes?°[12]   conceive

¿Por qué, pues has llagado
aqueste corazón, no le° sanaste?   = el corazón
Y pues me le has robado,
¿por qué así le dejaste,
45 y no tomas el robo° que robaste?   stolen item

Apaga° mis enojos,°   extinguish, troubles
pues que ninguno° basta° a deshacellos,°[13]   **nadie**, suffices, **deshacerlos**
y 'véante mis ojos,°   let my eyes see you
pues eres lumbre° dellos,°   light, **de ellos** (de los ojos)
50 y sólo para ti quiero tenellos.°   **tenerlos**

¡Oh cristalina° fuente,°   clear, spring
si en esos tus semblantes° plateados,°   countenance, silvery
formases 'de repente°   suddenly
los ojos deseados,
55 que tengo en mis entrañas° dibujados!°[14]   innermost recesses, sketched

¡Apártalos,° amado,   turn them (your eyes) away
que 'voy de vuelo!°[15]   I'm taking flight

---

[12] **Haciendo, porque mueras...** *Making arrows for yourself so that you die, (arrows made out) of what you receive, from what you conceive of your beloved?* The arrows are the experiences of Christ that the soul has; they are so powerful that they increase the desire of the soul to be with Him, in other words, die. As St. John explains in his commentary, the verb "concebir" is being used in the sense of mental conception, as well as the idea of the soul being impregnated with love and knowledge of God (Kavanaugh/Rodríguez, 502-504).

[13] **Apaga mis enojos...** *Snuff out my troubles, since nobody else can destroy them*

[14] **Si en esos...** *If only in that silvery countenance of yours you were to suddenly form the eyes I desire, the eyes that I have revealed to me in my innermost recesses*

[15] Compare to *Song of Solomon*, 6:4: "Turn away thine eyes from me, for they have overcome me." The soul asks Christ to withdraw his eyes from her sight, as the experience is of an overwhelming intensity; the soul then takes flight to commune with Christ outside the body.

Esposo:

Vuélvete,° paloma,°   return, dove
que el ciervo vulnerado°[16]   wounded
por el otero asoma,°   lets himself be seen
60 'al aire° de tu vuelo, y 'fresco toma.°   in the breeze, is cooled

Esposa:

¡Mi amado, las montañas,
los valles solitarios nemorosos,°   wooded
las ínsulas° extrañas,[17]   isles
los ríos sonorosos,°   sounding
65 el silbo° de los aires amorosos;°   whistling, loving

La noche sosegada,°   tranquil
'en par de° los levantes° de la aurora,°   at the same time as, east winds, s‖
la música callada,°   silent
la soledad° sonora,°   solitude, sounding
70 la cena que recrea° y enamora;°   delights, inspires love

Nuestro lecho° florido,°   bed, of flowers
de cuevas de leones enlazado,°   joined
'en púrpura tendido,°   hung with purple
de paz edificado,°   built
75 de mil escudos° de oro coronado!°[18]   shields, crowned

---

[16] Christ is symbolically depicted as a wounded stag. St. John writes that Christ shares in the wounds that his visitations have given to the bride-soul. If one feels wounded, so does the other, a sign of their unity (Kavanaugh/Rodríguez, 523).

[17] The reference here to "strange isles" has to do with a spiritualizing interpretation of the fact that on distant islands (perhaps in newly-discovered America) there are all sorts of strange new realities to discover, just as in the spiritual life there are new and strange things the human soul knows nothing of until it journeys further into God (Kavanaugh/Rodríguez, 527; 527n).

[18] This description of the bed comes from two places in the *Song of Solomon*: 1:16-17, and 3:9-10. In this latter reference, in some translations the word

'A zaga de° tu huella,°   following, footprint
las jóvenes discurren° al camino;   run
'al toque° de centella,°   at the touch, spark
al adobado° vino,   spiced
80   emisiones° de bálsamo° divino.[19]   outpourings, balsam

En la interior bodega°   wine cellar
de mi amado bebí, y cuando salía,
por toda aquesta° vega,°   esta, meadow
ya cosa no sabía[20]
85   y el ganado° perdí que antes seguía.   herd

Allí me dio su pecho,[21]
allí me enseñó ciencia° muy sabrosa,°   knowledge, delightful
y yo le di 'de hecho°   indeed
a mí, 'sin dejar cosa;°   without holding back anything
90   allí le prometí de ser su esposa.[22]

Mi alma se ha empleado,
y todo mi caudal,° en su servicio;   wealth

"chariot" is translated instead of "bed." St. John notes that the cave of lions in this stanza are the virtues in union with Christ, safe and secure as lion's dens (Kavanaugh/Rodríguez, 566).

[19] Literally, balsam is a substance that flows from certain trees or shrubs. Figuratively, it is anything that heals or soothes pain. In Christian doctrine, images of liquid outpouring are associated with the redemptive blood sacrifice of Christ.

[20] **Ya cosa no...** *I no longer was aware of anything*

[21] The "giving of the breast" must be interpreted in light of Christian tradition and symbolism; after Christ had died on the cross, "one of the soldiers pierced his side, and forthwith came there out blood and water" (John 19:34). That is, the blood sacrifice of Christ not only redeems, but also nourishes the soul that spiritually drinks of this outpouring.

[22] The promise to be the spouse of Christ is a moment of complete self-giving, a spiritual betrothal.

    ya no guardo° ganado, — look after
    ni ya tengo otro° oficio,° — any other, job
95 que ya sólo en amar es mi ejercicio.° — occupation

      Pues ya si en el ejido° — pasture
    de hoy más no fuere vista ni hallada,²³
    diréis que me he perdido;
    que andando enamorada,
100 'me hice perdidiza,° y fui ganada.° — got lost on purpose, won

      De flores y esmeraldas,° — emeralds
    en las frescas° mañanas° escogidas,° — cool, mornings, picked
    haremos las guirnaldas° — garlands
    en tu amor florecidas,° — blooming
105 y en un cabello mío entretejidas:° — interwoven

      En sólo aquel cabello
    que en mi cuello 'volar consideraste;° — you saw fluttering
    mirástele° en mi cuello, — you looked at it (my hair)
    y 'en él° preso° quedaste,° — in it (my hair), prisoner, you beca[me]
110 y en uno de mis ojos te llagaste.

      Cuando tú me mirabas,
    tu gracia en mí tus ojos imprimían;° — imparted
    por eso me adamabas,° — pursued
    y en eso merecían° — were worthy
115 los míos° adorar lo que en ti vían.°²⁴ — = los ojos míos, veían

      'No quieras despreciarme,° — don't scorn me

---

²³ **Pues ya...** *So now, if from today onwards I am no longer seen or found in the pasture.* The phrase "ya si" is connected to the phrase "de hoy más no," modifying the phrase "fuere vista ni hallada." The verb "fuere" is the future subjunctive of "ser," with "yo" as its subject.

²⁴ It is the imparting of grace by God that makes the soul worthy or deserving.

que si color moreno° en mí hallaste, [25]   dark
ya bien puedes mirarme,
después que me miraste,
120 que° gracia y hermosura en mí dejaste.[26]   **porque**

Cogednos° las raposas,°   Catch for us, foxes
que está ya florecida nuestra viña,°[27]   vineyard
'en tanto que° de rosas   while
hacemos una piña,°[28]   cluster
125 y 'no parezca nadie° en la montiña.°   let nobody appear, **montaña**

Deténte,° cierzo° muerto;°   hold still, north wind, killing
ven, austro,° que recuerdas° los amores,   south wind, you recall
aspira° por mi huerto,°   breathe, garden
y 'corran sus olores,°   let its fragrance spread
130 y pacerá° el amado entre las flores.[29]   will graze

Esposo:
Entrado se ha la esposa
en el ameno° huerto deseado,°   pleasant, desired (by the bride)
y 'a su sabor° reposa,°   in delight, rests
el cuello reclinado°   lying

---

[25] These lines are a rewriting of "I am black but comely... Look not (down) upon me, because I am black, because the sun hath looked upon me..." (Song of Solomon, 1:5-6).

[26] St. John writes that a glance from Christ imparts grace to the soul, erasing the darkness of sin, making it worthy to be looked upon (Kavanaugh/Rodríguez, 603).

[27] According to St. John's commentary, the vineyard in bloom is inner delight of God's love, and the foxes are the sensual appetites that will consume and destroy this (Kavanaugh/Rodríguez, 539).

[28] **En tanto que...** *While we make a bouquet of flowers.* The word "piña" means "cone" or "cluster." We've translated it as bouquet, presuming that such a liberty is within the realm of possibility.

[29] St. John explains that the garden is the soul; the bridegroom will "graze" on the love he finds there (Kavanaugh/Rodríguez, 543-544).

135 sobre los dulces brazos del amado.

    Debajo del manzano,°   apple tree
allí conmigo fuiste desposada,°   betrothed
allí te di la mano,
y fuiste reparada°   restored
140 donde tu madre fuera violada.°[30]   raped

    A las aves° ligeras,°   birds, swift
leones, ciervos,° gamos° saltadores,° deer, bucks, leaping
montes, valles, riberas,
aguas, aires, ardores°   warmths
145 y miedos° de las noches veladores,°[31] fears, wakeful

    Por las amenas liras°[32]   lyres
y canto° de serenas° os conjuro°[33]
que cesen° vuestras° iras°   song, **sirenas** = sirens, beseech
y 'no toquéis° al muro,°   cease, your, anger
                                don't touch, wall

---

[30] **Debajo del manzano...** *Under the apple tree.* The apple tree holds a double symbolism: it is the tree of crucifixion, which is the means by which Christ redeems and restores the human soul, which is then capable of consenting to spiritual betrothal and marriage, as well as the tree in the Garden of Eden, where Eve (the mother of all humanity) was seduced (here, "raped") by the serpent (Genesis 3:16).

[31] According to St. John, these correspond to the four passions, which are sorrow, hope, joy, and fear (Kavanaugh/Rodríguez, 554-555)   .

[32] A hand-held harp, a lyre is a stringed musical instrument of classical antiquity. The Spanish word "lira" also refers to a kind of poetic stanza consisting of heptasyllabic (seven-syllable) and hendecasyllabic (eleven-syllable) verses. Garcilaso de la Vega's "Canción V," featured earlier in this anthology, inaugurated the "lira" in Spanish poetry. Many subsequent Spanish poets, including St. John of the Cross in the poem you are currently reading, cultivated the "lira."

[33] In classical mythology, a siren is one of many sea nymphs (part woman, part bird) whose sweet, seductive singing lures sailors to their death.

150 porque la esposa duerma más seguro.[34]

Esposa:
Oh ninfas° de Judea,[35]   nymphs
'en tanto que° en las flores y rosales°   as long as, rose bushes
el ámbar° perfumea,°   amber, perfumes
morá°[36] en los arrabales,°   stay, outskirts
155 y 'no queráis° tocar nuestros umbrales.°[37]   do not seek, thresholds.

Escóndete, carillo,°   my dear one
y mira con tu haz° a las montañas,   face
y no quieras decillo;°[38]   **decirlo**
mas mira las compañas°   companions
160 de la que va por ínsulas extrañas.[39]

Esposo:
La blanca palomica°   little dove
al arca° con el ramo° se ha tornado,°   ark, branch, returned
y ya la tortolica°   little turtledove
al socio° deseado   mate

---

[34] St. John explains that the bridegroom is beseeching the passions to quiet themselves by means of the lyre (which fills the soul with sweetness) and the sirens' song (spiritual delight) and not touch the wall of peace, virtues and perfection around the garden where the beloved is sleeping. (Kavanaugh/ Rodríguez, 558-59)

[35] Judea is the southern region of the ancient land of Israel.

[36] The word "morá" is a non-standard, though common, "vos" command form of the verb "morar," meaning "to stay" or "to dwell" with the "d" dropped. In standard speech and writing this would be "morad"; St. John is being colloquial and rustic here by dropping the "d."

[37] According St. John, the nymphs of Judea are the lower passions, banished to the outskirts of the city, which is the soul (Kavanaugh/ Rodríguez, 547).

[38] **No quieras decillo...** *Don't say anything about it*

[39] See the footnote about the "ínsulas extrañas" for line 63.

165 en las riberas verdes ha hallado.[40]

En soledad vivía,[41]
y en soledad 'ha puesto° ya su nido,°   has made, nest
y en soledad la guía°   guides
'a solas° su querido,°   alone, lover
170 también en soledad de amor herido.°   wounded

Esposa:
Gocémonos,° amado,   Let us enjoy each other
y 'vámonos a ver° en tu hermosura[42]   let us go see ourselves
al monte o al collado°   hill
do mana° el agua pura;   flows
175 entremos 'más adentro° en la espesura.°   deeper, thicket

Y luego a las subidas°   high
cavernas° de la piedra nos iremos,   caverns
que están bien escondidas,°   hidden
y allí nos entraremos,
180 y el mosto° de granadas° gustaremos.°[43]   juice, pomegranates, we will taste

Allí me mostrarías°   would show

---

[40] These images are from the book of Genesis, chapter 8. Noah sends out a dove through the window of the ark, who at first returns empty-beaked; seven days later, he sends the dove out again, and she returns with an olive branch in her mouth (Genesis 8:11.) Here, the white dove is symbolic of the soul made pure by God's grace; in the *Song of Solomon*, 1:14, the bridegroom says his beloved has "dove's eyes." The olive branch is a sign that the flood waters have receded and thus is a sign of God's mercy. Turtledoves are significant in their single-minded desire for their mate, symbolic of how the soul should desire its mate, God (Kavanaugh/Rodríguez, 605-607).

[41] The subject of the verb is still the turtledove of the previous stanza.

[42] The soul becomes so like Christ that she will attain like beauty.

[43] In his commentary, St. John explains that, further up and further in to the mysteries of the experience of God, the pomegranate juice represents further delights to be had (Kavanaugh/Rodríguez, 617).

aquello° que mi alma pretendía,°⁴⁴   that thing, was seeking
y luego me darías
allí tú, vida mía,
185 aquello que me diste el otro día:⁴⁵

El aspirar° del aire,   breathing
el canto de la dulce filomena,°   nightingale
el soto y su donaire,°   charm
en la noche serena°   calm
190 con llama que consume y no 'da pena;°   cause grief

'Que nadie lo miraba,°   for no one was looking
Aminadab tampoco parecía,°   **aparecía**
y el cerco° sosegaba,°   siege, ended
y la caballería°   cavalry
195 'a vista de° las aguas descendía.°⁴⁶   at the sight of, descended

---

⁴⁴ In this clause, the subject is "alma" and the object is "aquello."
⁴⁵ The next stanza tells what the "aquello" of this stanza consists of.
⁴⁶ "Aminadab" is mentioned in *Song of Solomon* 6:12. He is an enemy, i.e. the Devil. Now that the soul is in such a state of perfection, this enemy does not show up to harass it; the "siege" mentioned is that of the passions, which are no longer assaulting the soul; the "waters" are the spiritual blessings flowing from the soul, at the sight of which the cavalry, which St. John identifies as the senses of the body. These senses are now sharing in the overflow of blessings by virtue of their proximity to the purified soul (Kavanaugh/Rodríguez, 628-630).

CANCIÓN II

La noche oscura[47]

Canciones del alma ° que 'se goza de °
haber llegado ° al alto estado ° de
la perfección, que es la unión con Dios,
por el camino de la negación ° espiritual.

soul, enjoys
having arrived, state

self-denial

En una noche oscura,
con ansias° en amores inflamada,[48]
(¡oh dichosa° ventura!)°
salí[49] sin 'ser notada,°
5   estando ya mi casa[50] sosegada.°

longings
happy, chance
being noticed
quiet

'A oscuras° y segura,
por la secreta escala° disfrazada,°
(¡oh dichosa ventura!)
a oscuras y 'en celada,°
10 estando ya mi casa sosegada.

in darkness
ladder, disguised

concealed

---

[47] In general conversation, people sometimes use the phrase "dark night of the soul" to refer to a particularly depressing, difficult, or troublesome period of one's life. While the phrase does not necessarily exclude these popular understandings, it has a technical theological meaning in the work of San Juan de la Cruz: the "dark night" refers to the soul's turning away from all things that are not God, even good and comforting things, in order to journey toward union with God. It is self-denial and self-purification. The stages of the soul's journey are depicted in the poem, and the relationship between the soul and God is portrayed as that between two lovers, a traditional Christian reading of the *Song of Solomon*, in Spanish, *El cantar de los cantares*.

[48] **En amores inflamada...** *Inflamed with love.* "Inflamada" is modifying "alma."

[49] The soul, realizing God's absence and her desire for him, begins her journey to him.

[50] The "house" of the soul is the body.

En la noche dichosa,
en secreto, que nadie me veía,
ni yo miraba cosa,°   anything
sin otra luz ni guía°   guide
15 sino° la° que en el corazón ardía.°   except, = **la luz**, burned

   Aquesta° me guiaba   = **esta** *luz*
más cierta° que la luz del mediodía,   surely
adonde me esperaba
quien yo bien 'me sabía,°51   I knew
20 en parte° donde 'nadie parecía.°   place, nobody could be seen

   ¡Oh noche que me guiaste!,
¡oh noche amable más que el alborada!,°   dawn
¡oh noche que juntaste
amado con amada,52
25 amada en el amado transformada!53

   En mi pecho florido,°   flowery
que entero para él solo se guardaba,
allí quedó dormido,
y yo le regalaba,°   caressed
30 y el ventalle° de cedros° aire daba.   = **ventarle** *fanning*, cedars

   El aire de la almena,
cuando yo sus cabellos esparcía,°   spread out
con su mano serena°54   serene

---

51 **Adonde me esperaba...** *To where the one whom I knew well was waiting for me*

52 The noun "amado" refers to God, and "amada" refers to the soul.

53 **Amada en amado...** *The beloved transformed into the lover.* The soul, through union with God, becomes a part of God. This doctrine is known as deification or apotheosis.

54 **Su mano serena...** *Its serene hand.* The "serene hand" belongs to the breeze.

en mi cuello hería,°[55]   wounded

35 y todos mis sentidos° suspendía.   senses

    Quedéme y olvidéme,
el rostro recliné sobre el amado,
cesó todo, y dejéme,[56]
dejando mi cuidado°   cares

40 entre las azucenas° olvidado.[57]   lilies

---

[55] According to St. John, "wounding" is a type of spiritual visitation in which God somehow touches the soul in such a way as to leave it more inflamed with passion for Him. It is not a wound that damages, but a purging fire that cauterizes and therefore heals and transforms (Kavanaugh/Rodríguez, 484).

[56] **Dejéme...** *I left myself.* The soul has abandoned all its worldly desires and now desires only her lover, i.e., God.

[57] The adjective "olvidado" is modifying "cuidado."

CANCIÓN III

Llama de amor viva[58]

Canciones del alma en la íntima comunicación
de unión de amor de Dios.

> ¡Oh llama de amor viva
> que tiernamente° hieres°[59]   tenderly, wound
> de mi alma en el más profundo centro!
> Pues ya no eres esquiva°[60]   distant
> 5   acaba° ya si quieres,   consummate
> ¡rompe la tela° de este dulce encuentro![61]   veil

---

[58] "Viva" is modifying "llama," not "amor," to give us *Living Flame of Love.*

[59] St. John's poetry often refers to the "wounds of love," visitations of Christ to the soul that leave the soul aflame with longing. See the note to line 4 of "Cántico espiritual," the note to line 34 of "Noche oscura" and Kavanaugh/ Rodríguez, 484, for further explanation.

[60] **Pues ya no...** *Since you are no longer distant.* According to St. John, this flame (which is Christ) was once distant to the soul, when it was in the state of purgation. Now, the soul has progressed to a state of spiritual union with Christ. (Kavanaugh/ Rodríguez, 648)

[61] **Rompe la tela...** *Tear the veil of this sweet encounter.* The word "tela" has been translated here as "veil," though a more literal rendering would be "cloth" or "fabric." We have chosen "veil" because in English it alludes to the rending, or tearing, of the veil in the temple in Jerusalem at the moment of Christ's death on the cross, recorded in Matthew 27:51, Mark 15:38 and Luke 23:45. The veil was a curtain separating the holiest area of the temple, the Holy of Holies, from the other areas; only the high priest could enter this holy chamber. The writer of the Epistle to the Hebrews likened Christ's sacrifice of his broken body to the rent veil: Christ provided a "new and living way, which he has consecrated for us, through the veil, that is to say, his flesh" (Hebrews 10:20). According to the writer of Hebrews, the tearing of the veil, analogous to Christ's body being crucified, symbolically provides access to God's presence for all, not just the High Priest. In the spiritual life, the soul necessarily has to progress to this point by purgation and illumination.

¡Oh cauterio° suave!°[62]
¡Oh regalada° llaga!°
¡Oh mano blanda! ¡Oh toque° delicado
10 que a vida eterna sabe°
    y toda deuda paga!°[63]
Matando, muerte en vida has trocado.

cautery, gentle
caressing, wound
touch
tastes of

¡Oh lámparas de fuego[64]
    en cuyos resplandores°
15 las profundas cavernas° del sentido,°[65]
que estaba oscuro y ciego,[66]
    con extraños primores°
color y luz dan junto a su querido!

splendors
depths, sense

delights

¡'Cuán manso° y amoroso°
20 recuerdas° en mi seno°
donde secretamente solo moras,°
    y en tu aspirar° sabroso°
de bien° y gloria lleno,[67]
cuán delicadamente 'me enamoras!°

how meek, loving
you awaken, breast
you dwell
breathing, delicious
blessings
you cause me to love you

---

[62] The word "cauterio" ("cautery" in English) is a surgical procedure in which a wound is treated ("cauterized") by applying a hot iron, needle or caustic substance. It is a way of purifying the wound. St. John equates it with the Holy Spirit (Kavanaugh/Rodríguez, 658).

[63] **Toda deuda paga...** *Pays all debt.* Christ's sacrifice is often spoken of as paying humanity's debts (Kavanaugh/Rodríguez, 666).

[64] The "lamps of fire" are God in his being and in his attributes (Kavanaugh/Rodríguez, 673).

[65] According to St. John, the deep caverns of sense are the intellect, will and memory (Kavanaugh/Rodríguez, 680-681).

[66] "Oscuro" and "ciego" modify "sentido."

[67] "Lleno" is modifying "aspirar."

Alonso de Ercilla (1533-ca. 1594)

ALONSO DE ERCILLA Y Zúñiga was born in Madrid into a noble family; his mother was a lady-in-waiting to the queen. As a boy he was a page to Prince Philip, who would later reign as Philip II. Like so many other Golden Age Spanish poets, he became a soldier and subsequently participated in the Spanish conquest of America, specifically Chile. He was later exiled to Peru. When he was about thirty years old, he returned to Spain, where he served as a courtier to Philip II and wrote about his adventures as a young soldier. He died at the age of 61 in Madrid.

The work Ercilla left, *La Araucana,* is an epic poem ("epopeya"). It is the first epic poem set in America, and one of the most esteemed epics in the Spanish language. We have included two fragments of it here and they are the only examples of epic poetry in this anthology. Epic poetry is generally a lengthy piece of narrative verse that tells of heroes and their exploits. In this case, the poem produced was based on Ercilla's personal experience in the conquest. *La Araucana* tells of how the Spanish subdued the indigenous people of Chile, known as the Mapuches or Araucans. The poem is full of admiration for these native Americans and their heroic resistance to Spanish domination. Their leader was Caupolicán, and Ercilla's idealized depiction of him no doubt ensured his immortality.

Ercilla y Zúñiga, Alonso de. *La Araucana.* Intr. Ofelia Garza de Del Castillo. México: Porrúa, 1992

Seguel, Gerardo. *Alonso de Ercilla. Fundador de la poesía en Chile y del pensamiento chileno.* Santiago de Chile: Ediciones Ercilla, 1940.

OCTAVAS REALES[1]

Descripción de Chile
    Chile, fértil provincia y señalada
en la región antártica famosa,
de remotas naciones respetada
por fuerte, principal° y poderosa;   noble
5 La gente que produce es tan granada,°   upstanding
tan soberbia,° gallarda° y belicosa,°   spirited, brave, aggressive
que no ha sido por rey jamás regida°   governed
ni a 'extranjero dominio° sometida.°   outside domination, subdued

Descripción de Caupolicán[2]
    Era este noble mozo 'de alto° hecho   fully
varón° de autoridad, grave y severo,   man
amigo de guardar° todo derecho,°   respect, rights
áspero° y riguroso, justiciero;°   harsh, fair
5 De cuerpo grande y relevado° pecho,   chiseled
hábil, diestro,° fortísimo y ligero,°   skilled, swift
sabio, astuto, sagaz,° determinado   shrewd
y en casos de repente reportado.°   calm

[de *La Araucana*]

---

[1] The two *octavas reales* (royal octaves) featured here come from Ercilla's lengthy narrative poem *La Araucana*, published in three parts (1569, 1578, and 1589). *La Araucana*, like other Renaissance epics, is a polished account of a historical event—in this case, Pedro de Valdivia's conquest of Chile and the Mapuche (Araucanian) indians on behalf of Spain.

[2] In the sixteenth century, during the Spanish conquest of Chile, Caupolicán emerged as the leader of the Mapuche resistance.

Miguel de Cervantes (1547-1616)

FAR MORE FAMOUS FOR his great novel *Don Quijote*, his novellas (*Novelas ejemplares*), and his drama than for his poetry, Miguel de Cervantes did write poetry that is worth reading. His importance in the Spanish literary tradition is comparable to that of Shakespeare's in the English-speaking world, and this fact alone makes his poetry worthy of consideration. Like Shakespeare, Cervantes's biography holds gaps that historians can only speculate about; however, what we do know for certain about Cervantes is far more interesting than anything we can make up.

Cervantes was born in Alcalá de Henares in 1547, the fourth of seven children. His father, Rodrigo de Cervantes, was a humble barber-surgeon, which is not at all the equivalent of being a doctor in today's terms. Also, Rodrigo was at least partially deaf. In a time and place where almost no societal accommodations for disabilities existed, Rodrigo would have been at a disadvantage in exercising his profession. As it was, it seems that Cervantes's father had other difficulties, such as malpractice suits, which often precipitated swift departures from various cities. The family moved around with frequency, and historians have not been able to track most of Cervantes's childhood. When Cervantes was around twenty years of age, he studied for a few months under the humanist scholar Juan López de Hoyos. The Cervantes family held the rank of *hidalgo*, or, minor nobility. It is possible that Cervantes's mother, Leonor de Cortinas, was descended from converts from Judaism.

Cervantes's first poems were published in Madrid in 1569 by López de Hoyos. Around this time, after wounding a rival in a duel, Cervantes fled to Rome, where he served in the entourage of a cardinal named Giulio Acquaviva. He became a soldier, fighting against the Turks in the Battle of Lepanto (1571) where he was gravely wounded and almost died. As a result of these injuries, he lost the use of his left hand and received the nickname, "el manco de Lepanto" ("the one-handed man of

Lepanto"). Cervantes took pride in his wounds and in his participation in what was felt to be the empire's finest moment. In 1575, as Cervantes attempted to return to Spain, his galley was attacked by pirates, and he was taken captive. He was held in Algiers for five years before being ransomed by a religious order, the Trinitarians. Cervantes's military experience in Lepanto and his captivity in Algiers appear in his later writings.

On his return to Spain, Cervantes devoted much of his energy to playwriting and to staging his plays, almost all of them now lost. He also wedded Catalina de Salazar, a union which produced no children, though Cervantes did have a daughter by another woman. In 1585, Cervantes published his first major work, the pastoral novel *La Galatea*.

Cervantes was often frustrated in his attempts to make a living and support his family. Eventually he was given the job of collecting funds for the Armada, which involved traveling over much of southern Spain. In 1590, Cervantes applied for a position in the New World, but his request was denied. However, he did receive an appointment as tax collector. But it was as a tax collector where Cervantes ran into difficulties and ended up in jail for a short period during the 1590s. While Cervantes came to enjoy wide acclaim for *Don Quijote* (Part One, 1605; Part Two, 1615), his *Novelas ejemplares* (1613), and several other works, he never achieved financial security, and was overshadowed by the wildly popular Lope de Vega. He died in 1616, a year after the publication of the second part of *Don Quijote*. His last work, *Los trabajos de Persiles y Sigismunda*, was published posthumously in 1617.

Cervantes embedded poetry within his prose narratives in a way that is both diverting and interesting. In this edition, we have included two verse works that appear in his novel *Don Quijote*.

Canavaggio, Jean. *Cervantes*. Trans. J. R. Jones. New York: Norton, 1991.

Lathrop, Tom, ed. *Don Quijote* by Miguel de Cervantes. Newark, Del.: Cervantes and Co., 2006

McCrory, Donald P. *No Ordinary Man. The Life and Times of Miguel de Cervantes.* London: Peter Owen, 2002.

SONETO[1]

Diálogo entre Babieca y Rocinante[2]
　—¿Cómo estáis, Rocinante, tan delgado?° — skinny
—Porque nunca se come, y se trabaja.
—Pues, ¿qué es de la cebada° y de la paja?° — barley, straw
—No me deja° mi amo° ni un bocado°. — leaves, master, bite

5　　—Andá,° señor, que estáis muy 'mal criado,° — Come on now, ill-mannered
pues vuestra° lengua de asno°[3] al amo ultraja°. — your, donkey, insults
　—Asno se es de la cuna° a la mortaja.° — cradle, funeral shroud
¿Queréislo° ver? Miraldo° enamorado.[4] — = lo queréis, = miradlo

　　—¿Es necedad° amar? —No es gran prudencia. — foolishness
10　—Metafísico° estáis. —Es que no como. — philosophical
—Quejaos° del escudero.° —No es bastante. — complain, squire

---

[1] This sonnet appears in the *Versos preliminares* ("Preliminary Verses") section of *Don Quijote*, just after the Prologue and before the story itself. It was customary for books, such as romances of chivalry, to contain poems in praise of the book and its characters; such poems were customarily written by people other than the book's author. In the case of *Don Quijote*, Cervantes mimics and parodies this practice by including several poems such as the sonnet featured here.

[2] *Don Quijote* mimics and makes fun of the heroic epic legends and books of chivalry that were so popular during the Spanish Golden Age. Specifically, *Don Quijote* burlesques the structure, language, plots, and characters of such legends and books. In effect, the knight (caballero) Don Quijote and his squire (escudero) Sancho Panza fall short of the idealized knights and squires of such texts. Rocinante, Don Quijote's horse, also falls short of the sturdy and robust horses of epic and romance. The prototype of such a horse was Babieca, the horse belonging to El Cid, the legendary hero of the Spanish *Reconquista*. In this sonnet, Cervantes imagines a conversation between El Cid's horse and Don Quijote's horse.

[3] The word "asno" also refers to a crude and ignorant person.

[4] Rocinante is referring to his master, Don Quijote, whose perceptions have been distorted by love.

¿Cómo me he de quejar en mi dolencia,°   pain
si el amo y escudero o mayordomo°   steward
son tan rocines° como Rocinante?   meager

[de *El ingenioso hidalgo Don Quijote de la Mancha*]

OVILLEJO

Versos de Cardenio[5]

¿Quién menoscaba° mis bienes?°   diminishes, well-being
                 Desdenes.°   disdain
Y ¿quién aumenta° mis duelos?°   increases, afflictions
               Los celos.°   jealousy
5 Y ¿quién prueba mi paciencia?
               Ausencia.

De ese modo, en mi dolencia
ningún remedio° 'se alcanza,°   remedy, is reached
pues me matan la esperanza
10 desdenes, celos y ausencia.

  ¿Quién me causa este dolor?
               Amor.
Y ¿quién mi gloria repugna?°   detests
               Fortuna.
15 Y ¿quién 'consiente en° mi duelo?   allows
               El cielo.

De ese modo, yo recelo°   suspect
  morir deste mal estraño,
pues se aumentan en mi daño,
20 amor, fortuna y el cielo.

  ¿Quién mejorará mi suerte?
             La muerte.
Y el bien de amor, ¿quién le alcanza?
             Mudanza.°   change

---

[5] In Book I of *Don Quijote*, when Don Quijote and Sancho Panza are wandering in a forest (the Sierra Morena), they hear a man singing these verses without instrumental accompaniment. The singer turns out to be a man named Cardenio, who fled to the forest in a fit of madness after believing that his beloved Luscinda had forsaken him for another man.

25 Y sus males, ¿quién los cura?

                             Locura.°   madness

De ese modo, no es cordura°   sanity

querer curar la pasión

cuando los remedios son

30 muerte, mudanza y locura.

[de *El ingenioso hidalgo Don Quijote de la Mancha*]

Luis de Góngora (1561-1627)

BORN IN THE ANDALUSIAN city of Córdoba, Luis de Góngora y Argote was the son of Francisco de Argote and Leonor de Góngora. Though his father held a prestigious position as *corregidor* (a provincial judge), Góngora's mother claimed more prestigious ancestry. Our poet, in effect, came to be known by his mother's more recognizable surname (and not by his father's surname, as was more common). After growing up in Córdoba, Góngora entered the University of Salamanca, where he studied civil and canon law. At this time, he developed his taste for literature and art, but also cultivated an interest in gambling, bullfighting, and other activities that the Church and society deemed profligate. By the time Góngora reached his mid-twenties, he had composed a great deal of poetry. Even at this early age, he was a poet of note: Miguel de Cervantes praised him in his pastoral novel *La Galatea* (1585). Soon after his university years, Góngora took minor orders toward the priesthood and became a prebendary (a kind of priest) at the Cathedral of Córdoba.

The attainment of a steady income in a holy office did not deter Góngora from pursuing his literary interests. As Góngora matured, his writing did too: in his late thirties, forties, and early fifties, Góngora perfected his signature poetic style. Characterized by latinisms, puns, erudite allusions, playful imagery, and convoluted syntax, this experimental style—now known as gongorism or *gongorismo*—is seen as the crux of the *culteranismo* movement of the seventeenth century. However, many influential writers, including Lope de Vega and Francisco de Quevedo, intensely disliked *culteranista* poetry, and worked to promote poetry that was more traditionally Garcilasan in style.

Góngora's two masterworks from this era—the *Soledades* and the *Fábula de Galatea y Polifemo* (1611-13)—became the special targets of anti-*culteranista* critics. For most of the rest of his life, Góngora engaged in literary feuds with the likes of Lope and Quevedo. Frequently, these

polemics became very personal in nature, as some antago-
nists—Quevedo in particular—lobbed accusations of sodomy and
converso descent against Góngora. Not unexpectedly, this polemic fueled
the creation of some of the wittiest and most satirical poetry ever written
in Spanish. It should be noted that many of Góngora's enemies devel-
oped great skill in *gongorista* poetic style, and gongorism remained
influential in Spanish poetry until the eighteenth century. It should also
be noted that Góngora never devoted himself exclusively to *culteranista*
poetry: he continued to practice a wide range of poetic styles and
registers throughout his career, and he also wrote some prose (most of
it lost) and drama (notably, *Las firmezas de Isabela*).

In 1617 Góngora was appointed chaplain to King Philip III. This
honor did not last long, however, as the king died in 1621. Subsequently,
Góngora unsuccessfully attempted to secure even more prestigious
positions at court. During these years, Góngora's penchant for gambling
and living beyond his means continued. His financial circumstances
became so dire, that in 1625 his residence in Madrid was put up for
auction. Góngora's personal and literary enemy, Francisco de Quevedo,
bought the house and proceeded to kick Góngora out of it. A year later,
still burdened with debt and newly burdened with a memory-impairing
illness, Góngora returned to Córdoba. He died in 1627.

Alonso, Dámaso. *La lengua poética de Góngora*. Madrid: CSIC, 1961

Collins, Marsha S. *The Soledades, Góngora's Masque of the Imagination*. Columbia
and London: U of Missouri P, 2002

Jammes, Robert. *La obra poética de don Luis de Góngora y Argote*. Trans. Manuel
Moya. Madrid: Castalia, 1987

SONETO LIV

De la brevedad° engañosa° de la vida   brevity, deceitful

     Menos solicitó° veloz° saeta   sought, swiftly
destinada señal,° que mordió° aguda;°[1]   target, nipped, sharply
agonal° carro por la arena muda°   competing, mute
'no coronó° con más silencio meta°[2]   did not achieve, goal

5   Que presurosa° corre, que secreta°   hastily, secretly
a su fin nuestra edad.[3] A quien lo duda,
fiera° que sea de razón desnuda,°   brute, stripped
cada 'Sol repetido° es un cometa.°[4]   day, warning sign

     Confiésalo° Cartago,° ¿y tú lo ignoras?[5]   = **Lo confiesa**, Carthage
10 Peligro corres, Licio, si porfías°[6]   persist
en seguir sombras y abrazar engaños.

     Mal te perdonarán a ti las horas:
las horas que limando° están los días,   eroding
los días que royendo° están los años.   gnawing away

---

[1] The noun "saeta" is the subject of the verb "solicitó," and "señal" is the direct object. The phrase "que mordió aguda" refers to "saeta."

[2] In these two verses, "carro" is the subject, "coronó" is the verb, and "meta" is the direct object.

[3] **Agonal carro... ...** *No competing chariot on the silent sand achieved its goal with more silence than our age has, which hastily and secretly runs towards its end*

[4] **A quien lo duda...** *For anyone who doubts it, even the brute that may be stripped of reason, each day is a warning sign*

[5] Carthage was an ancient city-state in North Africa. It was founded by the Phoenicians in the 9th century BC, but in the 2nd century BC it was destroyed by Rome during the last of the Punic Wars. In the 1st century BC Carthage was rebuilt by Julius Cæsar, but was destroyed in the 7th century by the Arabs.

[6] "Licio" is a man's name. Like many names in poems, "Licio" does not necessarily refer to a real person.

SONETO CIII

De un caminante ° *enfermo que 'se enamoró* °
donde fue hospedado °

    Descaminado,° enfermo, peregrino°
en tenebrosa° noche, con pie incierto°
la confusión pisando° del desierto,
voces° en vano dio, pasos sin tino.°[7]

 5   Repetido latir,° si no vecino,°
distinto° oyó de can° siempre despierto,°
y en pastoral° albergue° mal cubierto°
piedad° halló, si no halló camino.°[8]

    Salió el Sol, y entre armiños° escondida,°[9]
10 soñolienta° beldad con dulce saña°
salteó° al 'no bien° pasajero.°[10]

    Pagará el hospedaje° con la vida;
más le valiera errar° en la montaña
que morir 'de la suerte° que yo muero.[11]

Glosses (right margin): wanderer, fell in love; lodged; lost, wanderer; shadowy, unsure; treading; shouts, aim; barking, nearby; clear, dog, watchful; rustic, dwelling, roofed; hospitality, direction; ermine fur, shrouded; drowsy, fury; assaulted, ill, traveler; hospitality; straying; in the manner

---

[7] **La confusión...** *Treading the confusion of the desert, gave shouts in vain, steps without aim*

[8] **Y en pastoral...** *And in a poorly roofed, rustic dwelling, he found hospitality, if not direction*

[9] The ermine is a weasel with dark brown fur that changes to white in the winter.

[10] **Salió el Sol...** *The sun came out, and shrouded in ermine furs, a drowsy beauty with sweet fury assaulted the ill traveler*

[11] **Más valiera...** *It is better for him to stray in the mountains than to die in the manner in which I'm dying*

SONETO CLXV

Ilustre y hermosísima María,[12]
mientras se dejan ver a cualquier hora
en tus mejillas° la rosada° Aurora,°[13] cheeks, rosy, sunrise
Febo°[14] en tus ojos y en tu frente° el día;[15] the sun, forehead

5 Y mientras con gentil descortesía° impoliteness
mueve el viento la hebra° voladora°[16] threads, flying
que la Arabia en sus venas atesora° hoards
y el rico Tajo° en sus arenas cría;°[17] Tagus River, produces

Antes que, 'de la edad° Febo eclipsado° by time, extinguished
10 y el claro día vuelto en noche obscura,
huya la Aurora del mortal nublado;°[18] storm cloud

---

[12] As with most names in poetry, "María" does not necessarily refer to a real person. The famous verse "Ilustre y hermosísima María" originally comes from a lengthy poem ("Eclogue III") by Garcilaso de la Vega.

[13] In Roman mythology, Aurora was the goddess of the dawn. By extension, "Aurora" often refers to daybreak itself.

[14] In Greek mythology, Phoebus was Apollo, the sun god. By extension, "Phoebus" often refers to the sun itself.

[15] The nouns "Aurora," "Febo," and "día" are the subject of the reflexive "se dejan ver."

[16] The noun "viento" is the subject of the verb "mueve," and the noun "hebra" is the direct object.

[17] **Que la Arabia...** *Which Arabia hoards in its veins, and the rich Tagus produces in its sands.* Arabia is a peninsula in southwest Asia, between the Red Sea and the Persian Gulf. The Tagus is a river in the Iberian Peninsula, flowing west through central Spain and Portugal to the Atlantic Ocean. According to legend, both Arabia and the Tagus were reputed to contain some of the purest gold in the world.

[18] **Antes que, de la edad...** *Before (Phoebus extinguished by time and the bright day transformed into dark night) Aurora flees the deadly storm cloud.* In this clause, the phrase "de la edad.../...en noche obscura" is parenthetical and breaks up the main phrase.

Antes que lo que hoy es rubio° tesoro   golden
venza° a la blanca nieve su blancura:[19]   triumphs over
goza, goza, el color, la luz, el oro.[20]

---

[19] **Antes que lo que hoy...** *Before what today is a golden treasure triumphs over white snow with its own, imminent whiteness*

[20] All of the preceding clauses in this poem are subordinate to this sentence.

SONETO CLXVI

Mientras por competir con tu cabello,
oro bruñido° al sol relumbra° en vano;[21]　　　　burnished, shines
mientras con menosprecio° en medio el llano°[22]　　contempt, meadow
mira tu blanca frente° el lilio° bello;[23]　　　　forehead, white lily

5　Mientras a cada labio, por cogello,°　　　　= **cogerlo** *to kiss it*
siguen más ojos que al clavel° temprano;[24]　　carnation
y mientras triunfa con desdén° lozano°　.　　disdain, vigorous
del luciente° cristal tu gentil cuello:[25]　　shining

Goza cuello, cabello, labio y frente,
10　antes que lo que fue en tu 'edad dorada°[26]　golden youth
oro, lirio, clavel, cristal luciente,

No sólo en plata o viola° troncada°　　　violet, crushed
se vuelva, mas tú y ello juntamente
en tierra, en humo, en polvo, en sombra, en nada.[27]

---

[21] The noun "oro" is the subject of the verb "relumbra."

[22] **En medio el llano...** *In the middle of the meadow*

[23] The noun "frente" is the subject of the verb "mira," and "lilio" is the direct object.

[24] **Mientras a cada labio...** *While more eyes pursue each lip, to kiss it, than they do the early-blooming carnation*

[25] The noun "cuello" is the subject of the verb "triunfa," and the direct object is "cristal."

[26] The extended phrase "lo que fue.../...cristal luciente" is the subject of the verb "se vuelva." This verb is subjunctive because it follows "antes que." In the final two verses, the subject "tú y ello" also refers to "se vuelva."

[27] **Goza cuello...** *Enjoy your neck, hair, lips, and brow before all that was gold, lily, carnation, and shining crystal in your youth not only turns to silver or crushed violet, but you and it together become earth, smoke, dust, shadow, nothing*

LETRILLA XIX

Oveja °perdida, ven²⁸   sheep
sobre mis hombros, que hoy
no sólo tu pastor soy,
sino tu pasto ° también.²⁹   pasture

5   Por descubrirte mejor
     cuando balabas° perdida,   you were bleating
     dejé en un árbol la vida
     donde me subió el amor;³⁰
     si prenda° quieres mayor,°   pledge (sign of love), greater
10   mis obras hoy te la den.³¹

     Oveja perdida, ven
     sobre mis hombros, que hoy
     no sólo tu pastor soy,
     sino tu pasto también.

---

²⁸ The poem, told in the voice of Christ, is based on the parable of the Good Shepherd, found in Matthew 18, verses 10-14. In it, Jesus tells of the shepherd who owns one hundred sheep and notices that one has gone astray. He leaves the other ninety-nine sheep to search for the one lost one. It is analogous to the relationship between Christ, called the "Good Shepherd" in Christian tradition, and the lost human soul.

²⁹ The poetic speaker, in the voice of Christ, says that he is not only the "Pastor" (shepherd of the soul) but also the "pasture," that is, the very nourishment of the soul. This nourishment is at once spiritual, in that the soul can be nourished in prayer, and physical, in that the Eucharist that the faithful ingest in the Roman Catholic Mass is a physical substance, believed to be the literal body and blood of Christ. In this way the pastor (shepherd) is also the pasture (food).

³⁰ **Dejé en un...** *I left my life on a tree where love had put me.* The tree is the cross, on which Christ was crucified out of love for humanity.

³¹ **Si prenda quieres...** *If you want a greater pledge (sign) of love, let my works be it [that sign] for you*

15   Pasto al fin hoy tuyo hecho,[32]
     ¿cuál dará mayor asombro,°   amazement
     o el traerte yo en el hombro,
     o el traerme tú en el pecho?[33]
     Prendas son de amor estrecho°   close
20 que aun los más ciegos las ven.[34]

    Oveja perdida, ven
sobre mis hombros, que hoy
no sólo tu pastor soy,
sino tu pasto también.

---

[32] **Pasto al fin...** *At last today I am made your pasture*

[33] **¿Cuál dará mayor...** *What could be more amazing, the fact that I bear you on my shoulders or that you bear me in your breast (heart)?*

[34] These "prendas" (pledges, tokens, signs of love) are, first of all, Christ's sacrifice of himself on the cross, so great that even the blind can see them. The blind referred to are both the physically blind, cured by Christ in his earthly ministry, and those whose spiritual eyes, through grace, are opened to this truth. Then, the "prendas" also refer to Christ's act of carrying the lost sheep on his shoulders, and the possibility of being born in the heart of those who receive them; these are all an extension of the work on the cross.

LETRILLA XLVIII

Ándeme ° *yo caliente*   let me walk
y ríase la gente. °[35]   may people laugh

'Traten otros° del gobierno   may others deal
del mundo y sus monarquías,
mientras gobiernan mis días[36]
mantequillas y pan tierno,
5 y las mañanas de invierno
naranjada° y aguardiente,°   orangeade, brandy
  y ríase la gente.

Coma en dorada vajilla°   tableware
el Príncipe mil cuidados,[37]
10 como píldoras° dorados;[38]   pills
que yo en mi pobre° mesilla°   modest, little table
quiero más una morcilla°[39]   blood sausage
que en el asador° reviente,°   roasting spit, sizzles
  y ríase la gente.

---

[35] The phrase "Ándeme yo caliente" is very challenging to translate into English. The nineteenth-century poet Henry Wadsworth Longfellow renders the phrase as "Let me go warm and merry still." More recently, Elias Rivers translated the phrase as "Let me be wildly enthusiastic" (*Renaissance and Baroque Poetry of Spain*, 187) and Edward Friedman, L. Teresa Valdivieso, and Carmelo Virgillo render the phrase as "Let me get all worked up" (*Aproximaciones al estudio de la literatura hispánica*, 172). The full meaning of the phrase includes all of these nuances, and likely a few others.

[36] The noun "días" is the direct object of the verb "gobiernan."

[37] The noun "Príncipe" is the subject of the verb "coma," and "mil cuidados" is the direct object.

[38] The adjective "dorados" refers to the noun "cuidados."

[39] Other terms for "morcilla" in English are "blood pudding" and "black pudding." It is a dark sausage typically made from pig's blood, pork fat, and other ingredients.

15   Cuando cubra las montañas
de blanca nieve el enero[40]
tenga yo lleno el brasero°   hearth
de bellotas° y castañas,°   acorns, chestnuts
y quien las dulces patrañas°   old stories
20 del Rey que rabió° me cuente,[41]   went mad
    y ríase la gente.

    Busque° 'muy en hora buena°   Let seek, with my best wishes
el mercader° nuevos soles;[42]   merchant
yo conchas° y caracoles°   seashells, snails
25 entre la menuda° arena,°   fine, sand
escuchando a Filomena°[43]   nightingales
sobre el chopo° de la fuente,°   poplar, spring
    y ríase la gente.

    Pase a medianoche el mar,

---

[40] The noun "enero" is the subject of the verb "cubra," and "montañas" is the direct object.

[41] **Tenga yo...** *May I have the hearth full of acorns and chestnuts, as well as someone who may tell me the pleasant, old stories of the king who went mad*

[42] The noun "mercader" is the subject of the verb "busque," and "soles" is the direct object.

[43] The Spanish word "Filomena" derives from the Greek "Philomela." In classical mythology, Philomela, one of Procne's sisters, needed to travel to Thrace. Procne's husband, Tereus, agreed to escort Philomela. At journey's end, Tereus raped Philomela and cut out her tongue so that she could not betray him. However, Philomela wove a tapestry revealing Tereus's crime, and sent it to her sister. Out of revenge, Procne killed Itys (her son by Tereus), and served his corpse as a stew to Tereus. Procne then fled with Philomela, but when Tereus realized what had happened, he pursued them. When Tereus caught up with them, the two sisters begged the gods to save them. The gods responded and changed them to birds. In early versions of this myth, Procne was changed into a nightingale, and Philomela was changed into a swallow. However, in later versions of the myth (such as Ovid's influential *Metamorphoses*), Procne was changed into a swallow and Philomela was changed into a nightingale.

30 y arda° en amorosa llama,   let burn
    Leandro por ver su dama;°⁴⁴   beloved woman
    que yo más quiero pasar
    del golfo° de mi lagar°   gulf, winepress
    la blanca o roja corriente,°   stream
35   *y ríase la gente.*

    Pues Amor es tan cruel
    que de Píramo y su amada⁴⁵
    hace tálamo° una espada,°⁴⁶   wedding bed, sword
    do se junten ella y él;

---

⁴⁴ "Leandro" is the subject of the verbs "pase" and "arda." In classical mythology, the youth Leander swam the Hellespont river every night to visit his beloved Hero, a priestess of the goddess Aphrodite. Each night, Hero placed a lamp high up on the tower of the house where she lived; this enabled Leander to see while he swam. One stormy night, the wind extinguished the lamp's flame, and Leander consequently drowned. The next day, Hero discovered Leander's corpse at the base of her tower. In despair, Hero threw herself off the balcony.

⁴⁵ In classical mythology, Pyramus and Thisbe were two young lovers of Babylon who, against their parents' orders, conversed secretly through a crack in the wall which separated their houses. One day, frustrated by the physical separation imposed upon them, they made plans to meet each other later in the evening at the Tomb of Ninus, under a tall mulberry tree full of white berries. Thisbe arrived first, but fled when she saw a lioness nearby whose mouth was dripping with blood from a recent kill. As Thisbe ran away, her cloak fell, and the lioness chewed up and bloodied the cloak. Moments later, when Pyramus came upon the scene, he found Thisbe's mangled and bloody cloak. He carried the cloak over to the mulberry tree and lay it on the ground. Out of despair and guilt over Thisbe's presumed death, Pyramus drew his sword and killed himself; his blood spurted and changed the mulberries from white to red. Moments later, when Thisbe returned to the tomb in order to meet with her lover, she found Pyramus on the ground, bloodied and in the throes of death. Thisbe saw her bloodied cloak next to Pyramus, and knew what had happened. In turn, she took Pyramus's sword and plunged it into her heart, thus ensuring union with her lover in death.

⁴⁶ "Amor" is the subject of the verb "hace."

40 sea mi Tisbe un pastel
      y la espada sea mi diente,
          y ríase la gente.

Lope de Vega (1562-1635)

FÉLIX LOPE DE VEGA Carpio, known simply as Lope de Vega, was probably the greatest celebrity of the Spanish society of his time. During his lifetime, he was held in higher esteem than Cervantes was, though Cervantes is more famous now to the average person, mainly through the worldwide diffusion of the *Don Quijote* character. North American students should know that while Cervantes has often been compared to Shakespeare, Lope has also been the subject of this comparison. In one respect, Lope is a far more obvious parallel in that both he and Shakespeare were responsible for creating a national theater in their respective homelands; both writers wrote for mass appeal, not for an elite minority.

Lope's output was massive. He wrote at least several hundred plays, and possibly several hundred more, most of them totally in verse. In his plays he mixed traditional native Spanish poetic forms with the newer, more fashionable, cosmopolitan Italianate forms. He also wrote prodigious amounts of poetry of all sorts: lyric (both profane and religious), narrative, and dramatic. He experimented in all of the literary genres of the day and is hailed for his artistically innovative development of the *tragicomedia*, or tragicomedy. He explains his rationale for such a hybrid in his manifesto (again, in verse) titled *El arte nuevo de hacer comedias en este tiempo*. In this work, Lope breaks with the Aristotelian model of tragedy, rejecting the three unities of place, time, and action. The reduction of the typical play from five to three acts was another facet of Lope's theater. In the *Arte nuevo*, Lope says that his priority is entertaining the "vulgo" (the "common people") who pay to see his work. Lope is famous for claiming that he wrote plays merely for the income they brought him, but it is obvious that he took care with many (though not all) of his works to produce a polished product. Lope's literary style is characteristically affective, that is, meant to strongly affect the emotions of the public.

Lope was born in Madrid in 1562; he was a child prodigy who was writing poetry from a very young age and who wrote his first play at the age of twelve. He was from a humble family, but distinguished himself intellectually and artistically at the Jesuit *Colegio Imperial*. Dropping out of school, Lope joined the military and ended up being secretary to several important court officials. In 1588 he sailed on the expedition of the Invincible Armada, the quixotic enterprise whose mission, to depose England's Queen Elizabeth I, ended in shipwreck, failure, and national humiliation. Lope's ship was one of the few to return to Spain.

Lope's life was filled with romantic scandals and irregular entanglements. His first relationship, an affair with a young married actress named Elena Osorio, began at age seventeen when he was a theology student. After their breakup, he wrote such scandalous, vicious things about her and her family that he was exiled from Madrid for almost a decade. He later married twice and had many extramarital affairs which resulted in around a dozen children being fathered by him.

After his second wife's death, Lope was ordained a priest. It was fairly common for men of this class to take such action at such a juncture in their lives, though it is somewhat hard for moderns to take it seriously. Lope was a devout believer, though, in spite of his unchaste inclinations and behavior. We have included one of his most beautiful sacred poems in this volume, "Qué tengo yo, que mi amistad procuras?" In his later years, Lope suffered a series of personal misfortunes, including the death of several of his children, whom he loved with great passion and devotion. Shortly before Lope died, in 1635, his favorite daughter was abducted by her lover. The shock of this event may have precipitated his death. All Spain mourned his passing.

Hayes, Francis C. *Lope de Vega*. Boston: Twayne, 1967

Lázaro Carreter, Fernando. *Lope de Vega; introducción a su vida y obra*. Salamanca: Anaya, 1966

SONETO

Versos de amor, conceptos esparcidos[1]
engendrados° del alma en mis cuidados,   born
partos° de mis sentidos abrasados,°   offspring, burning
con más dolor que libertad nacidos;

5   Expósitos° al mundo en que perdidos,   abandoned
tan rotos anduvistes y trocados°[2]   changed
que sólo donde fuistes engendrados
fuérades por la sangre conocidos:

Pues que le hurtáis° el laberinto a Creta,   you steal
10 a Dédalo° los altos pensamientos,[3]   Dædalus
la furia al mar, las llamas al abismo,

---

[1] In this sonnet the speaker is addressing his "versos" and "conceptos," that is, the poem itself.

[2] **Tan rotos...** *So broken and changed you walked*

[3] According to classical mythology, Dædalus was an inventor, sculptor, and architect from Athens. His nephew, Talos, became his pupil, but proved so gifted that Dædalus got jealous and killed him. Sentenced to exile because of his crime, Dædalus fled to Crete where he became architect and sculptor at the court of King Minos. Minos's wife, Pasiphæ, fell in love with a bull, and gave birth to a son that was half human and half bull—the legendary Minotaur. At the King's request, Dædalus constructed a palace—the Labyrinth—to which the Minotaur would be confined. Later on, the heroic youth Theseus decided to fight the Minotaur, and with the help of his beloved Ariadne (the daughter of Minos and Pasiphæ), he succeeded: Theseus unrolled a ball of thread as he passed through the Labyrinth; after slaying the Minotaur, he exited the Labyrinth by following the unrolled thread. When Minos found out about this plot's success, he accused Dædalus of being an accomplice, and had him—and his son Icarus—imprisoned in the Labyrinth. But Dædalus made wings of wax for himself and his son, and they both flew away. Though Icarus flew too close to the sun and plummeted into the sea after his wings melted, Dædalus escaped safely.

Si aquel áspid° hermoso no os aceta,[4]   snake
dejad la tierra, entretened° los vientos,   play with,
descansaréis en vuestro centro mismo.[5]

[de *Rimas Humanas*]

---

[4] The "áspid" ("asp" or "snake") refers to the "mundo" to which the "versos" have been abandoned.
[5] **Descansaréis...** *You will rest in your proper place*

SONETO

Cuando me paro a contemplar mi estado
y a ver los pasos por donde he venido,
'me espanto° de que un hombre tan perdido   I get scared
a conocer su error haya llegado.[6]

5   Cuando miro los años que he pasado,
la divina razón puesta en olvido,
conozco que piedad° del cielo ha sido   compassion
no haberme en tanto mal precipitado.°[7]   hurled

Entré por laberinto tan extraño
10 fiando° al débil hilo de la vida   entrusting
el tarde conocido desengaño,[8]

Mas, de tu luz mi escuridad° vencida,°   = oscuridad, conquered
el monstruo° muerto de mi ciego engaño,[9]   monster
vuelve a la patria la razón perdida.[10]
[de *Rimas Sacras*]

---

[6] **A conocer...** *Has come to recognize his error*

[7] **Conozco que...** *...I realize that it has been due to Heaven's grace that I have not descended into the depths of evil*

[8] **Entré...** *I entered this truly strange labyrinth, trusting the weak thread of my life to lead me to the revelation which, at long last, I now understand.* At the court of King Minos, the architect Dædalus was commissioned to construct a palace—the Labyrinth—for the half-human, half-bull offspring (the Minotaur) resulting from a union between a bull and Pasiphæ, the wife of Minos. The Minotaur was confined to the Labyrinth, and every year Minos fed him seven young men and seven girls received as tribute from Athens. One year, the youthful Theseus offered himself voluntarily as one of the victims, and with the help of his beloved Ariadne (the daughter of Minos and Pasiphæ), he unrolled a ball of thread as he entered the Labyrinth, then killed the beast, and then exited the Labyrinth by following the path charted by the unrolled thread.

[9] **De tu luz...** *My darkness conquered by your light, the monster within killed by my blind deception*

[10] "Razón" is the subject of "vuelve."

SONETO XVIII

¿Qué tengo yo, que mi amistad procuras?
¿Qué interés° 'se te sigue,° Jesús mío,   benefit, redounds to you
que a mi puerta, cubierto de rocío,°   dew
pasas las noches del invierno escuras?[11]

5   ¡Oh, cuánto fueron mis entrañas° duras,°   feelings, hard
pues no te abrí![12] ¡Qué extraño desvarío°   absurdity
si de mi ingratitud el hielo frío
secó las llagas° de tus plantas° puras![13]   wounds, feet

¡Cuántas veces el ángel me decía:
10   «Alma, asómate° agora a la ventana,   go
verás con cuánto amor llamar° porfía°»!   knocking, he insists on

¡Y cuántas,° hermosura soberana,°   = cuántas *veces*, supreme
«Mañana le abriremos» respondía,
para lo mismo responder mañana![14]
[de *Rimas Sacras*]

---

[11] **Qué interés...** *What benefit is it to you, my Jesus, that drives you — covered in dew — to spend the dark nights of winter at my door?* The image of Christ calling at the door of the heart can be traced back to words attributed to him by the author of the book of Revelation in the Bible: "Behold, I stand at the door, and knock; if any man hear my voice, and open the door, I will come in...." (Revelation 3:20)

[12] **¡Oh, cuanto...** *Oh, how hard was my heart, that I did not open up to you!* The noun "entrañas" means "bowels" but we have rendered it here as "heart." In older forms of English and Spanish, the word "bowels" would have conveyed the sense of the seat of one's emotions; the word "heart" is what conveys that now.

[13] **¡Qué extraño desvarío...!** *What strange madness if the cold ice of my ingratitude dried up the wounds in your pure feet!* The noun "planta" refers specifically to the soles of the feet, but was often used generally to mean "foot." The wounds referred to are the wounds Christ suffered during his Crucifixion.

[14] **¡Y cuántas...** *And on how many occasions, Sovereign Beauty, did I respond "We will open [the door of the soul] to him tomorrow," only to say the same thing the following day?* The speaker is addressing or referring to Christ as the "Sovereign Beauty."

SONETO

Yo dije siempre, y lo diré, y lo digo,
que es la amistad el bien mayor humano;
mas, ¿qué español, qué griego, qué romano
nos ha de dar este perfeto amigo?

5   Alabo,° reverencio,° amo, bendigo°   *I praise, I deeply respect, I bless*
aquél a quien el cielo soberano
dio un amigo perfeto, y no es en vano;[15]
que fue, confieso,° liberal° conmigo.   *I confess, generous*

Tener un grande amigo y obligalle[16]
10 es el último bien, y, por querelle,
el alma, el bien y el mal comunicalle;[17]

Mas yo quiero vivir sin conocelle;
que no quiero la gloria de ganalle°   **= ganarle** *win his friendship*
por no tener el miedo de perdelle.

[de *La Circe*]

---

[15] **Aquél a quien...** *Him to whom sovereign heaven has given a perfect friend, and it is not in vain*

[16] When the word "le" functions as a direct object pronoun (more commonly rendered as the gender-specific "lo" and "la" in the Spanish-speaking world), it is an example of the linguistic phenomenon known as *leísmo.*

[17] **Tener...** *It is the ultimate good to have a great friend and oblige him, and for loving him, to communicate to him the good and evil of the soul*

SONETO

—Boscán, tarde llegamos. ¿Hay posada?°   lodging
—Llamad desde la posta,° Garcilaso.   hitching post
—¿Quién es? —Dos caballeros° del Parnaso.°[18]   gentlemen, circle of poets
—No hay donde nocturnar° palestra° armada.°[19]   to spend the night, place, prepared

5   —No entiendo lo que dice la criada.
Madona,° ¿qué decís? —Que 'afecten paso,°   Ma'am, you move on
que obstenta° limbos° el mentido° ocaso°   **ostenta**, borders, deceptive, sunset
y el sol depinge° la porción rosada.°[20]   paints, pink

—¿'Estás en ti,° mujer? —Negóse° al tino°   Are you alright, refused, good sense
10   el ambulante° huésped[21]—. ¡Que en tan poco   wandering
tiempo tal lengua entre cristianos haya!

Boscán, perdido habemos el camino;
preguntad por Castilla, que estoy loco
o no habemos salido de Vizcaya.°[22]   Basque Country

[de *El Laurel de Apolo*]

---

[18] Parnassus, now known as Liakoura, was a mountain in central Greece. In Greek mythology, Parnassus was the home of music and poetry.

[19] **No hay donde...** *There is no room here prepared for literary intellectuals to spend the night.* The woman's speech is supposed to be difficult to understand. In ancient Greece, a palestra was a public place for practice in wrestling and other competitive sports.

[20] **Que afecten paso...** *That you move on, as the deceptive sunset is showing its borders, and the sun is painting the pink portion*

[21] **Negóse al tino...** *It is the wandering traveler who has lost the way*

[22] The Basque Country, located in northeastern Spain and in southwestern France, is the homeland of the Basque language.

SONETO

Laméntase Manzanares °de tener tan gran puente[23]   the River Manzanares

(*Habla el río*)

    ¡Quítenme° aquesta puente que me mata,   remove from me
señores regidores° de la villa;   councilmen
miren que me ha quebrado una costilla;°   rib
que aunque me viene grande me maltrata!°   mistreats

5   'De bola en bola° tanto 'se dilata,°   from end to end, it spans
que no la° alcanza° a ver mi verde orilla;°[24]   = la *puente*, manages, riverbank
mejor es que la lleven a Sevilla,
si cabe en el camino de la Plata.[25]

    Pereciendo° de sed en el estío,°   dying, summer
10 es falsa la casual° y el argumento   chance occurrence
de que en las tempestades tengo brío.°   vigor

    Pues yo con la mitad estoy contento,
tráiganle 'sus mercedes° otro río   you
que le sirva de huésped de aposento.°   room

[de *Rimas humanas y divinas*]

---

[23] The Manzanares is a short and shallow river that flows through Madrid.

[24] In this verse, the noun "orilla" is the subject of the verb "alcanza a ver," and the direct object pronoun "la" refers to "la puente."

[25] Seville is a city in southwestern Spain, on the long and navegable Guadalquivir River. During the Golden Age, the city served as the chief port of call for ships headed to and returning from the Americas. The Camino de la Plata (the Silver Route), first developed by the Romans, was an important commercial route for Spain during the Golden Age. The route began in Seville and headed north via the regions of Extremadura and León.

SONETO

A Violante[26]

Un soneto me manda hacer Violante,
y en mi vida me he visto en tanto aprieto;°   straits
catorce versos dicen que es soneto,[27]
burla° burlando van los tres delante.°[28]   joke, previous

5   Yo pensé que no hallara consonante°   rhyme
y estoy a la mitad de otro cuarteto,°[29]   quatrain
mas° si me veo en el primer terceto,°[30]   but, tercet
no hay cosa en los cuartetos que me espante.°   scares

Por el primer terceto voy entrando,
10   y parece que entré con pie° derecho,°[31]   footing, proper
pues fin con este verso le voy dando.

Ya estoy en el segundo y aun sospecho
que voy los trece versos acabando;
contad si son catorce y ya está hecho.

[de *La niña de plata*]

---

[26] This sonnet appears in Lope's play *La niña de plata* (1617), which takes place in Seville. Three men—Chacón, Leonelo, and don Juan—are on the street, outside the house of doña Teodora. Their conversation turns to matters of poetry and poetic creation, and Chacón recites this sonnet.

[27] **Catorce versos...** *They say that fourteen verses is a sonnet.* The subject of "dicen" is a generic "they" or "people."

[28] **Burla burlando...** *The three previous [verses] go joking around*

[29] A "cuarteto" ("quatrain" in English) is a stanza consisting of four verses. The current stanza is a good example of a "cuarteto."

[30] A "terceto" ("tercet" in English) is a stanza consisting of three verses. The third and fourth stanzas of the poem are good examples of "tercetos."

[31] As is the case in many other poems, the word "pie" can refer at once to a person's foot, a person's footing, and poetic meter.

SONETO

¿Quién es amor? Infierno de la vida.
¿De quién nace? Del ciego atrevimiento.°   *daring*
¿De qué vive? El favor° es su alimento.°   *kindness, nourishment*
¿Qué fuerza° tiene? Estar al alma asida.°   *strength, seized*

5   ¿Da muerte amor? Amor es homicida.
¿Da vida amor? Mezclada con tormento.
¿Dónde asiste?° En el ciego entendimiento.   *is it present*
Pues, ¿algo tiene amor?[32] Gloria fingida.

¿Qué tiene bueno amor? Algún secreto.
10 Todo lo vence° amor, griegos y godos.°[33]   *conquers, Goths*
Nadie se escapa, el mundo está sujeto.°   *under its control*

¿Con qué engaña amor? De varios modos.
¡Oh amor, 'vuelve por ti!° Dime, ¿a qué efeto   *defend yourself*
todos te infaman° y te buscan todos?   *slander*

[de *La corona merecida*]

---

[32] The subject of this question is "amor."

[33] **Todo lo vence...** *Love conquers all, Greeks and Goths alike.* In Lope's time, Greeks were considered the historic progenitors of refined civilization, and Goths were reputed to be barbarous, warlike peoples.

Francisco de Quevedo (1580-1645)

FRANCISCO GÓMEZ DE QUEVEDO y Villegas was born in Madrid in 1580 into a wealthy, prominent, and distinguished family. He was educated by the Jesuits and studied at the universities of Alcalá and Valladolid; at a young age began to acquire a reputation as an excellent poet. Famous for his mastery of the Spanish language, from its most sublime to its most grotesque and nasty aspects, Quevedo was both esteemed and feared in his day for his rapier wit.

Quevedo's earliest ambition was not to become a famous poet, but to succeed in politics. He served the Duke of Osuna in Naples and Sicily, but later became entangled in intrigues and suffered accusations, arrest, and imprisonment. His tendency to write poems satirizing contemporary figures eventually led to his confinement in a monastery. Several of his barbs were aimed at the poet Góngora, whose *culteranista* style he despised; we have included one of these poems in this anthology, "A un hombre de gran nariz." Quevedo not only despised Góngora's poetry, he also nursed a personal animus towards him, mixed with (or perhaps mainly motivated by) a virulent anti-Semitism, as Góngora was thought to be of *converso* descent. The two poets had been in competition with each other since their youth. One of the ways in which Quevedo fought the gongorist tendency in poetry was by editing and publishing the poetry of Fray Luis de León, whose elegance and clarity Quevedo saw as the best weapon against the artifices, obscure latinisms, and circumlocutions of his enemy.

Quevedo's poetry is often said to belong to the *conceptista* tendency, the *concepto* (English: conceit) being what Elias Rivers calls a "metáfora violenta." Rivers discusses further the fact that while the *culteranista* and *conceptista* tendencies are often opposed to each other, all Baroque poetry shows both tendencies (*Poesía lírica*, 19).

Apart from poetry, Quevedo distinguished himself as a writer of literary, philosophical, moral, and political prose works. His best-known prose works today are the picaresque novel titled *La vida del Buscón llamado don Pablos* (1626), and the *Sueños* (1627), a series of scathingly satirical essays on Spanish society. Just like much of Quevedo's poetry, both of these works reflect a pervasive sense of the need for *desengaño*, that is, unmasking life's tangle of lies, appearances, and deceptions in order to arrive at the essence of truth. Most of Quevedo's works express preoccupation with the decadence and corruption of Spanish society, the sense of how time eventually gnaws at and erodes human life, and how everything is transitory and passing away. This outlook dovetails with Quevedo's personal philosophical orientation, Stoicism. Aside from his other accomplishments, he produced translations of the Stoic philosophers Epictetus and Seneca into Spanish.

Olivares, Julián. *The Love Poetry of Francisco de Quevedo: An Æsthetic and Existential Study*. Cambridge and New York: Cambridge UP, 1983

Schwartz Lerner, Lía. *Metáfora y sátira en la obra de Quevedo*. Madrid: Taurus, 1983

Walters, D. Gareth. *Francisco de Quevedo, Love Poet*. Washington, D.C.: Catholic U of America P, 1985

SONETO

Amor constante 'más allá de °la muerte   beyond

    Cerrar podrá mis ojos la postrera°   final
sombra que me llevare el blanco° día,   fair
y podrá desatar° el alma mía   release
hora a su afán° ansioso lisonjera;°[1]   desire, pleasing

5   Mas no, en esotra parte,° en la ribera,°   place, shore
dejará la memoria en donde ardía:°   burned with passion
nadar sabe mi llama la agua fría,
y perder el respeto a ley severa.[2]

    Alma a quien todo un dios prisión ha sido,[3]
10 venas que humor° a tanto fuego han dado,[4]   blood

---

[1] **Cerrar podrá mis...** *The final shadow may close my eyes and take away the fair day from me, and Pleasing Time may release my soul to its anxious desire.* The subject of "Cerrar podrá" is "la postrera sombra." "La postrera sombra" is also the subject of the clause "que me llevare el blanco día." "Llevare" is a future subjunctive. The subject of the final two lines is "hora," which is perhaps best conceived as "time" or "end," "hour" in a more poetic sense, e.g., his hour (time of death) has come. It is modified by, though it is separated from, the adjective "lisonjera."

[2] **Mas no, en...** *But it (my soul), will not abandon its memory, in which it burned with passion, on that other shore; my flame knows how to swim in cold waters (without being quenched), and disrespect the harsh law (of death).* The cold water mentioned implies Lethe, the river of oblivion in classical mythology. Those who had died and who then in the afterlife drank from these waters had their memories wiped clean of their former lives before being birthed into their new ones. The poet is refusing to submit to this.

[3] **Alma a quien...** *My soul, imprisoned by none other than a god.* This verse refers to the god of love, Cupid, as having been a prison to the poet. The phrase "todo un dios" may be translated as "nothing less than a god" or "no less than a god."

[4] **Venas que...** *My veins, whose blood fueled such a fire.* In the medical beliefs during Quevedo's lifetime, the humors were four different bodily fluids: blood,

medulas° que han gloriosamente ardido: marrow

Su cuerpo dejará, no su cuidado;
serán ceniza,° más tendrá sentido;   ash
polvo serán, mas polvo enamorado.[5]

---

phlegm, black bile and yellow bile. An excess or deficiency in any one of the humors produced an imbalance and made the body sick. Since the reference is to veins, we can translate "humor" as "blood" and, by extension, nourishment or fuel.

[5] **Su cuerpo dejará...** *(The soul) will leave its body behind, but not its concerns. They (the veins) will be ashes, but ashes that will still feel. It (the marrow) will be dust, but dust that remains in love.* The subject of "dejará" is "alma" from verse 9. The subject of "serán" in verse 13 is "venas," and the subject of "serán" in verse 14 is "medulas."

SONETO

*Significase ° la propia ° brevedad de la vida sin
pensar, y con padecer, ° salteada ° de la muerte*

    Indicates, intrinsic
    suffering, attacked

Fue sueño ayer, mañana será tierra.°
¡Poco antes nada, y poco después humo!
¡Y destino° ambiciones,° y presumo
apenas punto° al cerco° que me cierra!°6

    grave

    I make, ambitious plans
    a dot, wall, encloses

5   'Breve combate° de importuna° guerra,
en mi defensa, soy peligro sumo,
y mientras con mis armas me consumo,
menos me hospeda° el cuerpo que me entierra.°7

    skirmish, pressing

    hosts, buries

Ya no es ayer, mañana no ha llegado;
10 hoy pasa y es, y fue, con movimiento
que a la muerte me lleva despeñado.°8

    headlong

Azadas° son la hora y el momento
que 'a jornal° de mi pena y mi cuidado
cavan° en mi vivir° mi monumento.°10

    shovels9
    paid by the day
    dig, **vida**, tomb

[de *Poemas metafísicos*]

---

6 **Y presumo...** *And I presume to do grand things, being hardly a point on the wall that imprisons me*

7 **En mi defensa...** *In my defense, I am the greatest danger to myself, and while I use my own weapons to destroy myself, my body becomes less of a host and more the thing that buries me*

8 **Que a la...** *That plunges me headlong over the cliff to death*

9 An "azada" is a hoe—a garden implement used to cut, scrape, and dig. Since the poet is emphasizing the digging function of the tool, we have decided that "shovels" might convey the poet's meaning better than "hoes."

10 **Azadas son la ...** *The hours and the moments are diggers, paid a day's wage in the currency of my grief and cares, digging my tomb in the ground of my existence*

SONETO

Retrato °de Lisi que traía en una sortija °11   portrait, ring

En breve° cárcel traigo aprisionado°   cramped, imprisoned
con toda su familia de oro ardiente
el cerco° de la luz resplandeciente°   circle, shining
y grande imperio del Amor cerrado.[12]

5   Traigo el campo que pacen° estrellado°   graze, starry
las fieras altas° de la piel° luciente°13   celestial, fur, shining
y a escondidas del cielo y del Oriente,°   rising sun
día de luz y parto° mejorado.[14]   birth

Traigo todas las Indias en mi mano,
10   perlas que, en un diamante, por rubíes,
pronuncian con desdén° sonoro° yelo.°15   disdain, sound (adj.), = **hielo**

---

[11] **Retrato de Lisi...** *Portrait of Lisi, which he wore in a ring..* Like many women's names in poems, "Lisi" is a pseudonym. This poem is about a miniature portrait of a woman contained in a ring. It was common at this time, for those who had the means, to make miniature drawings or paintings of loved ones and encase them in rings, locket-style pendants, or brooches. Note that "traer" can have different meanings, including "bring," "carry," "bear," "wear," and "keep."

[12] **En breve cárcel...** *In a cramped jail cell I keep, imprisoned, with its whole family of fiery gold, the ring of shining light, and Love's great empire locked within.* The "cramped jail" ("breve cárcel") is the ring holding the miniature portrait depicting Lisi.

[13] The "fieras altas" ("celestial beasts") are the animal constellations in the sky. They are located ("escondidas") in a higher sphere than the sun and planets. The speaker is, in effect, placing his love for Lisi on a very exalted plane.

[14] **Traigo el campo...** *I carry about the starry field that celestial beasts graze; in secret from Heaven and the sunrise, (I carry) a better day-light and day-birth.*

[15] **Traigo todas...** *On my hand I wear all the Indies: pearly teeth that, set in a diamond, pronounce ice-words with disdain through ruby lips.* The phrase "todas las Indias" refers to all of the wealth (precious gems, etc.) of the Indies.

Y razonan tal vez fuego tirano,
relámpagos° de risa carmesíes,°   lightning bolts, crimson
auroras,° galas,° y presunción del cielo.[16]   rose-colored dawns, jewels

[de *Poemas amorosos*]

---

[16] **Y razonan...** *And, sometimes utter forth tyrannical fire, crimson lightning-bolts of laughter, rose-colored dawns, heaven's fine dress and presumption.* The subject of the verb "razonar" is still the "perlas" of the last stanza.

SALMO[17]

Enseña cómo todas las cosas avisan °   warn
de la muerte

Miré los muros de la patria mía,
si un tiempo fuertes, ya desmoronados, °   crumbling
de 'la carrera de la edad° cansados,   the race of time
por quien caduca° ya su valentía. °[18]   is faltering, bravery

5   Salíme al campo; vi que el sol bebía
los arroyos° del hielo desatados, °   streams, melted
y del monte° quejosos° los ganados, °   woodland, complaining, herds c
que con sombras hurtó su luz al día.[19]

Entré en mi casa; vi que, amancillada, °   defaced
10 de anciana habitación° era despojos; °[20]   dwelling, rubble
mi báculo, ° más corvo° y menos fuerte.   walking stick, bent

Vencida de la edad sentí mi espada,
y no hallé cosa en que poner los ojos,
que no fuese recuerdo° de la muerte. [21]   reminder

[de *Heráclito cristiano*]

---

[17] A psalm is a sacred poem, song, or hymn, such as those found in the Book of Psalms in the Old Testament. Note that this psalm is essentially a sonnet.

[18] **Por quien...** *Because of which their courage is now faltering.* The "por quien" is not referring to any person, but rather to the condition of the walls. "Caducar" means to grow senile, expire or deteriorate.

[19] **Y del monte...** *And the herds of cattle complaining about the mountain who stole the light from their day with its shadow*

[20] **Entré en mi...** *I entered my house; I saw it was the rubble of an old, defaced dwelling*

[21] **Vencida de la...** *I felt my sword overcome by age, and I didn't find anything to set my eyes on that wasn't a reminder of death.*

SONETO

A un hombre de gran nariz[22]

Érase° un hombre a una nariz pegado,°   there once was, stuck
érase una nariz superlativa,°   exaggerated
érase una alquitara° 'medio viva,°[23]   alembic, half-alive
érase un 'peje espada° mal barbado;°   swordfish, bearded

5   Eera un 'reloj de sol° 'mal encarado,°   sundial, ugly-looking
érase un elefante 'boca arriba,°   face up
érase una nariz sayón° y escriba,°   executioner, scribe
un Ovidio Nasón mal narigado.[24]

   Erase el espolón° de una galera,°[25]   heavy spur, warship
10 érase una pirámide de Egito,[26]

---

[22] This sonnet satirizes the poet Luis de Góngora (1561-1627). In his later years, Góngora's poetry became progressively more experimental with thickly layered metaphors, Latin-style word order, invented words, and other techniques. Quevedo was one of the most vocal critics against Góngora's experimental style.

[23] **Alquitara medio viva...** *An alembic, half-alive.* An alembic was a type of still, an apparatus used in chemical distillation. A long beak-like cap was fastened to the top of the bottle, and the outline of the thing could give the impression of a person with an incredibly long nose.

[24] **Un Ovidio Nasón...** *A big-nosed Ovid poorly nosed.* This is a reference to the classical Roman poet Publius Ovidius Naso, commonly known as Ovid, the author of the *Metamorphoses*. His surname, Naso, is similar to the Spanish word "nasón," meaning "big nose." "Narigado" is an invented word, based on "narigón," an adjective meaning "big-nosed."

[25] A warship often had a heavy, beak-like spur (formally called a "ram") connected to the bow. This device was used to ram and penetrate the hull of an enemy ship during hostilities.

[26] The Pyramids of Ancient Egypt were, and still are, celebrated for their magnificent size.

las doce tribus de narices era;[27]

Érase un naricísimo infinito[28]
muchísima nariz, nariz tan fiera,°   beastly
que en la cara de Anás[29] fuera delito.°[30]   crime

---

[27] **Las doce tribus...** *The twelve tribes of noses.* An allusion to the twelve tribes of Israel, probably an anti-semitic remark.

[28] **Naricísimo infinito...** *Infinite nositude.* Seeing as Quevedo coined new words for this poem, we are following suit.

[29] **Que en la...** *That on the face of Annas it would be a crime.* Annas was the father-in-law of Caiaphas, the Jewish high priest who questioned Jesus after his arrest (John 18:13).

[30] There are different versions of this final tercet. We admit we have chosen the most linguistically accessible one. For an assessment of the various versions of the poem, see Roger Moore's "Erase un hombre a una nariz pegado. The Enigma of the Second Tercet," *Romance Quarterly* 42.1 (1995): 39-46.

SONETO

A Roma sepultada° en sus ruinas[31]   buried

    Buscas en Roma a Roma ¡oh peregrino!°   pilgrim
y en Roma misma a Roma no la hallas:
cadáver° son las que ostentó° murallas°   corpse, bragged, city walls
y tumba de 'sí proprio° el Aventino.[32]   = **sí propio** *itself*

5   Yace° donde reinaba° el Palatino[33]   It lies, reined
y limadas° del tiempo, las medallas°   worn away, medals
más se muestran 'destrozo a las batallas°   destruction of battles
de las edades que 'blasón latino.°[34]   glory of ancient Rome

    Sólo el Tibre° quedó, cuya corriente,[35]   the Tiber River
10 si ciudad la regó,° ya sepultura   watered
la llora° con funesto° son° doliente.°[36]   mourns, mournful, sound, sorrowful

    ¡Oh Roma en tu grandeza, en tu hermosura,
huyó lo que era firme° y solamente   stable
lo fugitivo permanece y dura!°[37]   endures

---

[31] The rise and fall of Ancient Rome is a common theme in the Renaissance and Spain's Golden Age.

[32] **Cadáver son las...** *The walls it (Rome) flaunted are a corpse, the Aventine a tomb for itself.* The Aventine is one of the Seven Hills of Rome, and it was a strategic commercial and military site.

[33] The subject of "yace" is Rome. The Palatine is another of the Seven Hills of Rome. Many powerful and wealthy Romans lived on the Palatine.

[34] **Y limadas del...** *And worn away by time, the medals reveal themselves to be more the destruction wrought by the battles of the ages than the glory of ancient Rome.*

[35] The Tiber is the river that runs through Rome.

[36] **Sólo el Tibre...** *Only the Tiber is left, whose current, if it once watered Rome as a city, now cries over it as a tomb with mournful, sorrowful tones*

[37] **Lo que era...** *What was firm has gone away, and only what is fleeting remains and endures*

SONETO

¡Ah de la vida!

"¡Ah de la vida!°"...¿Nadie me responde?   Hey, life!
¡Aquí de° los antaños° que he vivido!³⁸   Come back here, past years
La Fortuna mis tiempos 'ha mordido;°   has gnawed away at
Las Horas mi locura las esconde.³⁹

5   ¡Que sin poder saber cómo ni adónde,
la salud y la edad° se hayan huido!   youth
Falta° la vida, asiste° 'lo vivido,°   is absent, is present, the past
y no hay calamidad que no me ronde.°⁴⁰   threaten to return

Ayer se fue; mañana no ha llegado;
10 hoy se está yendo sin parar 'un punto;°   for a moment
soy un fue, y un será, y un es cansado.⁴¹

En el hoy y mañana y ayer, junto
pañales° y mortaja,° y he quedado   diapers, funeral shroud
presentes sucesiones de difunto.°⁴²   dead man

[de *Poemas metafísicos*]

---

³⁸ The poet is calling out to the past years of his life, seeing them slip away quickly.

³⁹ The noun "locura" is the subject of "esconde." The word "las" (i.e., "Las Horas") is the direct object.

⁴⁰ **Y no hay calamidad...** *And there is no calamity that does not threaten to return to me.* "Rondar" is in the subjunctive because its antecedent is negative/nonexistent.

⁴¹ **Soy un fue...** *I am a "was," a "will be," and a tired "is"*

⁴² **He quedado presentes...** *I am nothing but the current stage of a dead man*

LETRILLA

Poderoso caballero es don Dinero

Una letrilla[43] satírica

Madre, yo al oro 'me humillo°   humble myself
él es mi amante y mi amado,
pues, de puro enamorado,
'de contino° anda amarillo;°   always, pale
5 que pues, doblón° o sencillo,°[44]   doubloon, coin of lesser value
hace todo cuanto quiero,
poderoso caballero
es don Dinero.

Nace en las Indias honrado,°   honorably
10 donde el mundo le acompaña;
viene a morir en España,
y es en Génova enterrado°[45]   buried
Y pues quien le trae al lado
Es hermoso, aunque sea fiero,°   ugly
15 *poderoso caballero*
es don Dinero.
Es galán y es 'como un oro,°   neat as a pin
'tiene quebrado el color,°   he's discolored

---

[43] A letrilla is a poem or song which consists of a stanza alternating with a short refrain that is the same words as the opening lines, in this case the phrase "Poderoso caballero es don Dinero."

[44] The "doblón" ("doubloon" in English), a coin made entirely of gold, weighed twice as much as the "dobla," another kind of golden coin. Compared to the "doblón," the "dobla" held lesser value, and thus was an example of a "simple" coin (that, is, a "sencillo").

[45] This is the path of money: the wealth of gold and other precious metals came from the American colonies, "died" in Spain (i.e., disappeared in funding the many wars in Europe), and was buried in Genoa (a center of banking).

persona de gran valor,
20 tan cristiano como moro.°   Muslim
Pues que da y quita el decoro°   chastity
y quebranta° cualquier fuero,°   breaks, law
poderoso caballero
es don Dinero.

25   Son sus padres principales°   illustrious people
y es de nobles descendiente,
porque en las venas° de Oriente°[46]   veins, the East
todas las sangres son reales;[47]
y pues es quien hace iguales
30 al duque y al ganadero,°[48]   cattle rancher
poderoso caballero
es don Dinero.

Mas, ¿a quién no maravilla°   amaze
ver en su gloria 'sin tasa°[49]   limitless
35 que es lo menos de su casa
doña Blanca de Castilla?[50]
Pero, pues da al bajo° silla   low-born person

---

[46] The word "venas" refers to the process of the circulation of blood, but also alludes to terrestrial sources of precious metals such as gold, silver, and copper. The word "Oriente" refers to Asia, including the Near East. The Phoenicians, a Near Eastern culture that reached parts of coastal Spain, introduced money, in the form of coins, to Europe.

[47] In Golden Age Spain, a "real" was a kind of silver coin.

[48] **Es quien hace...** *He is the one who makes the duke and the cattle rancher equals*

[49] The word "tasa" has several financial meanings, such as "price" and "rate."

[50] A "blanca" was a copper coin of very little value. The daughter of Alfonso VIII of Castile and the wife of Louis VIII of France, doña Blanca of Castile (1188-1252) was twice the regent (interim ruler) of France as she waited for her son, Louis IX, to reach the age at which he could legally become king.

Y al cobarde hace guerrero,°[51]   warrior
poderoso caballero
40 *es don Dinero.*

   Sus 'escudos de armas° nobles   coats of arms
son siempre tan principales,
que sin escudos reales[52]
no hay escudos de armas dobles;[53]
45 y pues a los mismos robles°   oak trees
da codicia° su minero,°[54]   envy, origins
poderoso caballero
es don Dinero.

   Por importar en los tratos°   dealings
50 y dar tan buenos consejos,[55]
en las casas de los viejos
gatos° le guardan de gatos.°   moneybags, thieves
Y pues él rompe° recatos°   conquers, young women's modesty
y ablanda° al juez más severo,   softens up
55 *poderoso caballero*
es don Dinero.

   Y es tanta su majestad
(aunque son sus duelos hartos°)   sufficient
que con haberle hecho cuartos°   quarters

---

[51] **Pues da al...** *Since he gives the low-born person a seat (at the table of the socially important) and turns cowards into warriors*

[52] The "escudo real" was a type of coin used in Quevedo's Spain. This stanza presents a play on the various meanings of the word "escudo": shield, coat of arms, coin.

[53] **Sin escudos reales...** *Without escudos reales (money) there would be no double (i.e. two-faced, fraudulent) coats of arms*

[54] **A los robles...** *His origins even cause oak trees to be envious.* Money's lineage is older even than the oak trees.

[55] **Por importar...** *Because he's so important in dealings, and gives such good advice*

60 no pierde su autoridad;[56]
   pero, pues da calidad°   status
   al noble y al pordiosero,°   beggar
   poderoso caballero
   es don Dinero.

65   Nunca vi damas ingratas°   ungrateful
   a su gusto y afición°   taste
   que a las caras de un doblón
   hacen sus caras baratas;[57]
   y pues 'las hace bravatas°   he boasts to them
70 desde una bolsa° de cuero,   purse
   poderoso caballero
   es don Dinero.

   Más valen[58] en cualquier tierra
   (¡mirad 'si es harto sagaz!°)   how wise he is
75 sus escudos[59] en la paz
   que rodelas° en la guerra.   round shields
   Y pues al pobre le entierra
   y hace proprio al forastero,°[60]   foreigner
   poderoso caballero
80 *es don Dinero.*

---

[56] **Que con haberle...** *Even when divided into quarters, he doesn't lose his authority.* The word "cuarto" here means "quarter," as in a fraction, and the coin of the same name. It was a coin of little value, though still legal tender; hence, it didn't lose its authority.

[57] **Que a las caras...** *When they (the ladies) see the sides of a doubloon coin, they make their own faces cheap.* The sense of these verses depends on a wordplay involving different meanings of the word "cara." It can mean "face," "dear," and "beloved," as well as the obverse side of a coin (the one displaying the head of the ruler). When the ladies see this *cara,* they apply make-up on their own.

[58] The subject of the verb "valen" is "escudos," in verse 75.

[59] The poet is still indulging in wordplay with the various meanings of the word "escudo."

[60] **Y hace proprio al...** *And he (Sir Money) makes the foreigner his own.* In other words, Sir Money turns the foreigner into a citizen.

Pedro Calderón de la Barca (1600-1681)

CALDERÓN WAS ONE OF the brightest lights of Spanish Golden Age culture; he was Lope de Vega's natural successor as the premier playwright of his day, and his work possesses a philosophical breadth and depth achieved by few even in such a brilliant age as his was. Like Lope, his dramatic work is almost entirely in verse; he shows similarities with Góngora in his *culteranista* style and wordplay.

He was born in Madrid in 1600 to a prominent family and studied theology in preparation for the priesthood at the universities of Alcalá and Salamanca. He dropped out of school for military service in Italy and Flanders. Upon his return he served King Philip IV at his court in Madrid and eventually enjoyed official patronage of his work. All of the financial resources of the crown were put at his disposal, as was the theater at the new palace, the Buen Retiro. Calderón was appointed its director in 1635. This new theater enabled more mythological content and fantastical stories, with spectacular visual effects, singing, and dancing. Calderón's theater helped develop the *zarzuela*, Spain's national light opera.

These new developments made departing from strictly realistic art possible in order to explore and develop philosophical themes, such as the conflict between free will and predestination. We have included a speech from one of Calderón's plays, *La vida es sueño* (1635). It is the soliloquy of Prince Segismundo, who has been imprisoned by his father, King Basilio of Poland. Basilio took this action on the basis of dire astrological omens that accompanied his son's birth; his interpretations of these omens were such that they predicted Segismundo would be one of the cruelest rulers ever known. To avoid this destiny, Segismundo was raised away from society. Treated like a beast, the outcast prince almost becomes one, until he exercises his moral freedom to "obrar bien," or, do the right thing. In a sense, he represents the orthodox Christian view of every human being who, born in a state of Original Sin, is in a beastly state until receiving the light of grace. In this speech, from Act One, Scene Two, Segismundo appears, according to the stage directions, in chains and wearing animal skins.

Even with his great success as a court playwright and director, Calderón returned to military service whenever necessary. In 1637 he became a knight of the Order of Santiago; in 1642, he was wounded in battle at Constanti and thereafter retired from military service. In 1651, he was ordained to the priesthood, and died in Madrid in 1681. His death has been said to mark the end of the Spanish Golden Age, but such a viewpoint does not take into account that Sor Juana was still alive and writing in Mexico. Nevertheless, his passing was most definitely a sign of cultural twilight.

Calderón de la Barca, Pedro. *La vida es sueño.* Ed. Vincent Martin. Newark, Del.: Cervantes and Co., 2003

Gerstinger, Heinz. *Pedro Calderón de la Barca.* Trans. Diana Stone Peters. New York: Frederick, 1973.

Wardropper, Bruce, ed. *Critical Essays on the Theatre of Calderón.* New York: New York University Press, 1965.

SOLILOQUIO

¿Tengo menos libertad?[1]

Apurar,° cielos, pretendo,°   to examine, I seek
'ya que° me tratáis así°   since, thus
qué delito° cometí[2]   crime
contra vosotros, naciendo;
5 aunque si nací, ya entiendo
qué delito he cometido:
bastante° causa ha tenido   more than enough
vuestra justicia y rigor,[3]
pues el delito mayor
10 del hombre es haber nacido.

Sólo quisiera saber
para apurar mis desvelos°   restlessness
(dejando a una parte, cielos,
el delito de nacer),
15 qué más os pude ofender[4]
para castigarme más.   punish me
¿No nacieron los demás?
Pues si los demás nacieron,
¿qué privilegios tuvieron
20 que yo no gocé jamás?

---

[1] This soliloquoy comes from Calderón's most famous play, *La vida es sueño* (1635). The speaker is King Basilio's son, Segismundo. Due to ominous events and predictions upon Segismundo's birth, Basilio acted to maintain a shroud of secrecy over his son's existence. In effect, Segismundo was raised clandestinely, under lock and key. In this soliloquy, Segismundo laments his life of captivity and confinement.

[2] **Apurar, cielos...** *Heaven, since you treat me this way, I seek to understand what crime I have committed*

[3] **Bastante causa...** *Your justice and severity have had more than enough grounds (to treat me this way)*

[4] **Qué más...** *In what other way I have managed to offend you*

Nace el ave, y con las galas°   finery
que le dan belleza suma,
apenas es flor 'de pluma°   feathery
o ramillete° con alas,   cluster of flowers
25 cuando las etéreas° salas°   heavenly, chambers
corta° con velocidad,⁵   flies through
negándose° a la piedad°   denying himself, comfort
del nido° que deja en calma;   nest
¿y teniendo yo más alma,
30 tengo menos libertad?

Nace el bruto,° y con la piel°   beast, fur
que dibujan° manchas° bellas,   design, spots
apenas signo° es de estrellas   sign
(gracias al docto° pincel°)⁶   expert, artist's brush
35 cuando atrevida° y cruel   daring
la humana necesidad
le enseña a tener crueldad,
monstruo de su laberinto;⁷
¿y yo, con mejor instinto,
40 tengo menos libertad?

---

⁵ **Cuando las etéreas...** *When he flies through the chambers of heaven*
⁶ **Nace el bruto...** *Born is the beast, and with a coat of fur decorated with beautiful spots (thanks to the most expert of artistry), he is almost a representation of the stars above*

⁷ In classical mythology, on the island of Crete, Pasiphæ (the wife of King Minos) mated with a bull; the result was a son who was half-human, half-bull—that is, a Minotaur. The Minotaur was ordered enclosed in a palace (the Labyrinth) built by the architect Dædalus. Each year, King Minos received seven young men and seven girls as tribute from Athens, and these youths were fed to the Minotaur. One year, a heroic young man named Theseus offered himself as one of seven boys for the Minotaur, but he in fact devised a strategy to kill the Minotaur. With the help of Ariadne, the daughter of Minos and Pasiphæ, Theseus unfurled a ball of string as he entered the heart of the Labyrinth, killed the Minotaur, and then exited the Labyrinth by following the string back outside.

Nace el pez, que no respira,
aborto° de ovas° y lamas,°   freak, algae, mud silts
y apenas, bajel° de escamas,°   small boat, scales
sobre las ondas° 'se mira,°8   waves, is seen
45 cuando a todas partes gira,°   thrashes
midiendo° la inmensidad   measuring
de tanta capacidad°   expanse
como le da el centro° frío;   deep sea
¿y yo, con más albedrío,°   free will
50 tengo menos libertad?

Nace el arroyo, culebra°   snake
que entre flores 'se desata,°   flows
y apenas, sierpe° de plata,   serpent
entre las flores 'se quiebra,°   it noisily crashes
55 cuando músico celebra
de los cielos la piedad,°   grace
que le dan majestad°   dignity
del campo abierto a su huida;°9   flow
¿y teniendo yo más vida
60 tengo menos libertad?

En llegando a esta pasión,°   intense suffering
un volcán, un Etna hecho,°10   erupting
quisiera sacar del pecho
pedazos del corazón.
65 ¿Qué ley, justicia o razón,
negar° a los hombres sabe   deny
privilegio tan suave,°   kind
excepción° tan principal,°   privilege, great

---

8 **Nace el pez...** *Born is the fish, which does not breathe, a freak of algae and mud silts; a small vessel with scales, he is barely seen above the waves*
9 **Cuando músico...** *...When, like a musician, it celebrates heaven's grace for giving it the dignity of open space for its onward flow*
10 Mount Etna is an active volcano in eastern Sicily.

que Dios le ha dado a un cristal,°   body of water
70 a un pez, a un bruto y a un ave?

[de *La vida es sueño*]

Sor Juana Inés de la Cruz (ca. 1651-1695)

SOR ("SISTER") JUANA WAS born in what today is called Mexico, and lived there her entire life. At the time, though Mexico was a Spanish colony (the Viceroyalty of New Spain), it was geographically and culturally a distinct entity. In this way, Sor Juana can be said to be Mexican. However, Spanish peninsular culture was nonetheless pervasive at many levels in Colonial Mexico, and its presence in New Spain's political, intellectual, and religious life was specifically palpable. Positioned thus at the juncture of two cultural systems, Sor Juana is often included in anthologies of both Spanish and Spanish-American literature. She is considered one of the great poets of Spanish literature, but she also wrote plays and devotional works; she made the occasional foray into theology, which was not safe territory for anybody in the Counter-Reformation era, least of all for women. It was her theological scholarship defending the rights of women that made her a heroine of feminists; it is her evident accomplishment in such a wide variety of fields of knowledge that makes her a model scholar and notable human being.

Born to an unmarried woman near the small village of Nepantla, Sor Juana later achieved an unlikely and unpredictable level of international stardom. She was baptized Juana Inés Asbaje de Ramírez. Her father was a Spanish soldier of Basque origin and her mother was Mexican. Sor Juana was what we would call today a child prodigy, showing uncommon intellectual accomplishment in various fields as a very young girl, dazzling the professors of her day. She started her schooling (which was private tutoring at home) at the age of three and soon became known in the region for her intellectual precociousness. While still a child, she went to live with her aunt and uncle in the capital, where she was presented at court and became a well-known figure in high society. For the most part, Sor Juana was self-taught, higher education not being open to women in those days. She learned Latin, which was the main means of being able to read the important scientific, philosophical, and theological works of the day. Sor Juana also could write in Basque (perhaps learned from her father), Portuguese, and Náhuatl (the language of the Aztecs and their subjugated peoples).

Sor Juana made her profession as a nun of the Order of St. Jerome in 1669. The convent afforded her the opportunity to continue her studies and exercise her intellectual gifts, including her gift for poetry. Aside from her poetry, she is often known for her "Respuesta a Sor Filotea de la Cruz." The "respuesta" is, as the word indicates, a response to a letter from one "Sor Filotea" (in reality the Bishop of Puebla writing under a pseudonym), critical of Sor Juana's intellectual pride in daring to criticize the sermon of a Portuguese Jesuit. Sor Juana's response to Sor Filotea is simultaneously a defense of the right of women to exercise their intellectual gifts, a short intellectual autobiography, and a demonstration of sound rhetorical and argumentative techniques. The exchange with "Sor Filotea" is generally thought to have had a chilling effect on Sor Juana as she withdrew from public life shortly thereafter—but there are various interpretations of the emotional impact that this reprimand had on her.

Sor Juana died in an epidemic in 1695. Her works had recently been published in Spain with the title of *Inundación Castálida*. Before her death, she had given away her library and musical instruments, apparently as part of a special penance undertaken to celebrate the renewal of her vows on the twenty-fifth anniversary of her profession as a nun.

Kirk Rappaport, Pamela. ed. *Sor Juana Inés de la Cruz: Selected Writings*. New York: Paulist Press, 2005

Paz, Octavio. *Sor Juana, or, The Traps of Faith*. Trans. Margaret Sayers Peden. Cambridge, Mass.: Belknap, 1988.

Sabat de Rivers, Georgina, ed. *Inundación Castálida*. Madrid: Castalia, 1982.

SONETO

Éste que ves, engaño colorido °   colorful

Procura °desmentir °los elogios °   she tries, to deny, praises
que a un retrato °de la Poetisa °   portrait, female poet
inscribió °la verdad, que llama pasión.[1]   wrote

Éste que ves, engaño colorido
que del arte ostentando° los primores   displaying
con falsos silogismos° de colores[2]   syllogisms
es cauteloso° engaño del sentido;   crafty,

5   Éste, en quien la lisonja° ha pretendido°   flattery, tried
excusar° de los años los horrores,[3]   to exempt
y venciendo° del tiempo los rigores,   conquering
triunfar de la vejez y el olvido

Es un vano 'artificio del cuidado,°   careful trick
10   es una flor al viento delicada,
es un resguardo° inútil para el hado;°   safeguard, fate

Es una necia° diligencia° errada,°   useless, effort, failed
es un afán° caduco° y, 'bien mirado,°   desire, failed, correctly viewed
es cadáver, es polvo, es sombra, es nada.

---

[1] The praises that the poet is attempting to deny are the flattering aspects of a portrait of herself. She does so by writing the truth.

[2] A syllogism is a kind of logical argument central to deductive reasoning. An example of a basic syllogism is: *All humans are mortal; All politicians are humans; All politicians are mortal.* In Sor Juana's time, the word "silogismo" was also sometimes used to refer to false, deceptive arguments.

[3] **Éste, en quien...** *This (portrait), in which flattery has tried to exempt (its subject, the poet) from the ravages of the years.* The demonstrative pronoun "éste" refers to the portrait; "en quien" should be translated "in which," also referring to the portrait.

SONETO

Rosa divina que en gentil cultura °

                                            cultivation

En que da moral censura a una rosa,
y en ella a sus semejantes °⁴

                                            fellow roses

    Rosa divina que en gentil cultura
eres, con tu fragrante sutileza, °   subtlety
magisterio° purpúreo° en la belleza,   lesson, purple
enseñanza° nevada° a la hermosura;   example, snowy

5   Amago° de la humana arquitectura,   sign
ejemplo de la vana gentileza, °   gentility
en cuyo ser unió naturaleza,
la cuna° alegre y triste sepultura:⁵   cradle

    ¡Cuán altiva° en tu pompa,° presumida,° arrogant, splendor, conceited
10 soberbia,° el riesgo° de morir desdeñas,°   proud, risk, disdain
y luego desmayada° y encogida°   fainting, shrinking

    De tu caduco° ser das mustias° señas,°   failing, withered, gestures
con que tu docta° muerte y necia° vida,   learned, foolish
viviendo engañas y muriendo enseñas!

---

⁴ **En que da...** *In which she expresses moral condemnation of a rose, and in it (this condemnation), (condemns) its fellow roses.* In poetry, the rose (or any flower in bloom) is often a symbol of youth, beauty, or both.

⁵ **En cuyo ser...** *In whose (the rose's) being nature joined the cheerful cradle and the gloomy tomb*

REDONDILLAS

Hombres necios que acusáis

Arguye ° de inconsecuentes ° el gusto °   she argues, illogical, pleasures
y la censura ° de los hombres que en   condemnations
las mujeres acusan lo que causan. [6]

Hombres necios que acusáis
a la mujer sin razón°   grounds
sin ver que sois la ocasión°   cause
de lo mismo que culpáis:°   criticize

5   Si con ansia° sin igual   passion
solicitáis° su desdén,   you seek
¿por qué queréis que obren bien
si 'las incitáis° al mal?   provoke them

   Combatís° su resistencia   You break down
10   y luego, 'con gravedad,°   in all seriousness
decís que fue liviandad°   moral looseness
lo que hizo la diligencia.°   your (men's) efforts

   Parecer° quiere el denuedo°   to resemble, bravery
de vuestro parecer° loco   way of thinking
15   al niño que pone el coco°   bogeyman
y luego le tiene miedo.[7]

   Queréis, con presunción necia,
hallar a la que buscáis,
para pretendida,° Thais,   in pursuit

---

[6] **Arguye de inconsecuentes…** *She argues that the pleasures and condemnations of men who blame women for that which they (men) cause are illogical*

[7] **Parecer quiere el…** *The bravery of your crazy way of thinking is similar to that of a child who pretends there's a bogeyman and then gets frightened of it*

20 y 'en la posesión,° Lucrecia. [8]   *once possessed*

    ¿Qué humor° puede ser más raro   *mood*
que el que, falta de consejo,
él mismo empaña° el espejo,   *mists up*
y siente que no esté claro?[9]

25   Con el favor y el desdén
'tenéis condición igual,°   *you're all alike*
quejándoos, si os tratan mal,
burlándoos,° si os quieren bien.[10]   *mocking*

    Opinión,° ninguna° gana;   *in reputation, = ninguna mujer*
30 pues la que más 'se recata°   *acts prudently*
si no os admite,° es ingrata,°   *allow, ungrateful*
y si os admite, es liviana.°   *unchaste*

    Siempre tan necios andáis
que, 'con desigual nivel,°   *inconsistently*
35 a una culpáis° por cruel   *you blame*
y a otra por fácil culpáis.

    ¿Pues cómo ha de estar templada°[11]   *tempered*

---

[8] **Para pretendida, Thais...** *When you're chasing her, you want her to be like Thais, but once you get her, you want her to be like Lucretia.* "Pretender" means "to try to get." Thais was a famously seductive and powerful woman who convinced Alexander the Great to burn the city of Persepolis. Lucretia was a Roman noblewoman who committed suicide after being raped. She is often held up as an example of sexual purity and virtue.

[9] **¿Qué humor puede...** *What frame of mind could be stranger than that of a man who, lacking good advice, mists up the mirror and then regrets that it's not clear?*

[10] **Con el favor...** *[Whether women treat you] with favor or disdain, you're all alike, complaining if they treat you well, mocking if they love you well.* Something to remember is that "burlarse" can mean "scorn," "sneer," and "mock," but also, "seduce," with the implication of abandonment afterwards.

[11] **¿Pues cómo ha de...** *Well, how is she to be tempered...?*

la que vuestro amor pretende,°   seeks
si la que es ingrata, ofende,
40   y la que es fácil, enfada?°   angers (you)

    Mas, entre el enfado y pena°   sorrow
que vuestro gusto° refiere,°   whim, reveals
bien haya la que no os quiere,
y quejaos 'en hora buena.°   as much as you like

45   Dan vuestras amantes° penas   loving
a sus libertades alas,[12]
y después de hacerlas malas
las queréis hallar muy buenas.

    ¿Cuál mayor culpa ha tenido
50   en una pasión errada:°   sinful
la que cae 'de rogada°   because she is begged
o el que ruega 'de caído?°   because he is fallen

    ¿O cuál es más de culpar,
aunque cualquiera mal haga:
55   la que peca° por la paga   sins
o el que paga por pecar?

    Pues, ¿para qué os espantáis
de la culpa que tenéis?
Queredlas cual° las hacéis   in the way that
60   o hacedlas como buscáis.[13]

    'Dejad de solicitar,°   stop wooing
y después, con más razón,

---

[12] **Dan vuestras amantes…** *Your loving sufferings give wings to their (women's) liberties.*

[13] **Queredlas cual las…** *Either love them the way you've made them, or make them into what you're seeking*

acusaréis° la afición   reproach
de la que 'os fuere a rogar.°[14]   is going to woo you

65   Bien con muchas armas fundo°   I base my opinion
que lidia° vuestra arrogancia,   fights
pues 'en promesa e instancia°   with promises and entreaties
juntáis diablo, carne° y mundo. [15]   flesh

---

[14] **Dejad de solicitar...** *Quit wooing, then you'll be in a better position to reproach the woman who is courting your affections.* The verb "fuere" is the future subjunctive of "ir."

[15] **Bien con muchas...** *Well-founded is my opinion that your arrogance fights with many arms, for with promises and entreaties you unite the devil, the flesh and the world*

ROMANCE
A la Encarnación[16]

	Que hoy[17] bajó° Dios a la tierra	descended
	es cierto; pero más cierto	
	es, que bajando a María,°	Virgin Mary
	bajó Dios a mejor cielo.[18]	
5	Por obediencia del Padre	
	se vistió de carne el Verbo,°[19]	
	mas tal, que le pudo hacer	
	comodidad° el precepto.°[20]	comfort, commandment
	Conveniencia° fue de todos	suitable thing
10	este divino misterio,	
	pues el hombre, de fortuna,	
	y Dios mejoró de asiento.°[21]	seat
	Su sangre le dio María	
	'a logro,° porque 'a su tiempo,°	for a profit, in turn
15	la° que recibe encarnando	= la *sangre*

---

[16] *A la Encarnación*... To the Incarnation. This *romance* has been written in honor of the Incarnation, which signifies Jesus Christ the Son of God taking on human form (flesh, "carne") for the redemption of the human race. By extension this feast also honors his Mother, the Blessed Virgin Mary.

[17] The "hoy" referred to is the feast-day of the Incarnation, March 25th.

[18] The "mejor cielo" ("better heaven") is the womb of the Virgin Mary.

[19] *Se vistió*... The Word clothed himself in flesh. One of the ways Christ is referred to in the Christian tradition is as the "Word made flesh"; this reference can be found in the Gospel of John, 1:14: "And the Word was made flesh, and dwelt among us..."

[20] **Por obediencia del**... Through obedience to the Father (God), the Word (Jesus) clothed Himself in flesh, but in such a way as to make the command a comfortable place (i.e., Mary's womb)

[21] **Conveniencia fue de**... It was a suitable thing for everybody, since man bettered his fortune and God bettered his seat (throne). The verb "mejoró" is implied in the phrase "el hombre, de fortuna," with "el hombre" as the subject and "fortuna" the object.

restituya redimiendo;[22]
si ya no es que, para hacer
la redención, 'se avinieron,°   they came to an agreement
dando moneda la Madre
20 y poniendo el Hijo el sello.°[23]   seal
Un arcángel a pedir
bajó su consentimiento
guardándole, en ser rogada,
de reina los privilegios. [24]
25 ¡Oh grandeza de María
que cuando usa el Padre Eterno
de dominio° con su Hijo,   command
use con ella de ruego!
A estrecha° cárcel reduce   cramped
30 de su grandeza lo inmenso
y en breve morada cabe

---

[22] **Su sangre le...** *Mary gave him her blood, for a profit, so that the blood he receives in incarnating, he may give back in redeeming*

[23] **Para hacer la...** *They came to an agreement in order to carry out the redemption, the Mother giving coin and the Son putting his seal (upon it).* The words "redemption" and "redeem" are now mostly employed as theological terms, but are also used in relation to coupons, vouchers, and other means of exchange. Redemption is a type of purchase, but when it comes to the Christian faith, it often means one of the specific nuances of paying a ransom for a hostage, i.e., humanity in bondage to sin, and by extension, the Devil. The "seal" is what would be affixed to a contract agreement, which would bind the person who used it. In ancient times up through the early modern age, a seal would be an impression made in wax, often by a special ring worn by the authorized person. In this case, the contract is between Mary and the Son, and the latter binds himself to the agreement with the seal.

[24] **Un arcángel a...** *An archangel descended to request her consent, preserving with it (the consent) her privileges as queen because she (gave her consent when she) was asked.* The archangel referred to here is Gabriel. The feast of the Incarnation is also known as the feast of the Annunciation, when the archangel Gabriel came to Mary to tell her that she was to be the mother of Jesus (Luke 1:26-38.) Mary's consent is a much-celebrated topic in Christian culture.

quien sólo cabe en sí mesmo.[25]

VILLANCICO VI[26]

A Santa Catarina de Alejandría[27]

¡Víctor,° víctor Catarina,   = **vítor** *hurray*
Que con su ciencia° divina   knowledge
Los sabios ha convencido,[28]
Y victoriosa ha salido
5 Con su ciencia soberana°   supreme
De la arrogancia profana°   worldly
Que a convencerla ha venido![29]
¡Víctor, víctor, víctor!

De una mujer se convencen
10 todos los sabios de Egipto,
para prueba de que el sexo
no es esencia en lo entendido.°   rational mind
¡Víctor, víctor!

Prodigio° fue, y aun milagro;   marvel
15 pero no estuvo el prodigio
en vencerlos, sino en que

---

[25] **Quien sólo cabe...** *The one who fits only within himself.* This is referring to Jesus.

[26] "Villancico" usually means a Christmas carol but it can refer more generally to a hymn.

[27] St. Catherine of Alexandria (ca. 287-305) was a very learned and scholarly young woman who lived in Alexandria, Egypt, and who was martyred by the Roman emperor Maximin.

[28] Catarina is the subject of "ha convencido" and the "sabios" are the object of the verb.

[29] "Arrogancia profana" is the subject of "ha venido a convencerla."

ellos se den por vencidos.[30]
¡Víctor, víctor!

¡Qué bien se ve que eran sabios
20   en confesarse rendidos.°   surrendered
que es triunfo el obedecer°   obedience
de la razón el dominio!°[31]   rule
¡Víctor, víctor!

Las luces de la verdad
25   no se obscurecen° con gritos;°   = oscurecen *darken*, shouts
Que su eco sabe valiente
Sobresalir° del ruido.°   stand out, noisy quarrels
¡Víctor, víctor!

No se avergüenzan° los sabios   get ashamed
30   de mirarse convencidos
porque saben, como sabios,
que su saber es finito.
¡Víctor, víctor!

Estudia, arguye y enseña,[32]
35   y es de la Iglesia servicio,°   of service
que no la quiere ignorante°   unknowledgeable
El que racional la hizo.[33]
¡Víctor, víctor!

¡Oh qué soberbios° vendrían,   proud

---

[30] **Pero no estuvo...** *But the marvel was not in beating them, but in their giving up*

[31] **Qué bien se...** *How well it can be seen that they were wise in confessing themselves vanquished; what a triumph it is to obey the rule of reason!*

[32] The subject of all three verbs is Catarina.

[33] **Que no la...** *The one (God) who made her rational doesn't want her ignorant*

40 al juntarlos Maximino!³⁴
 Mas salieron admirados°   astonished
 Los que entraron presumidos.°   conceited
 ¡Víctor, víctor!

 Vencidos, con ella todos
45 La vida dan al cuchillo.³⁵
 ¡Oh cuánto bien 'se perdiera°   would have been lost
 si docta no hubiera sido!
 ¡Víctor, víctor!

 Nunca de varón ilustre
50 triunfo igual habemos visto;³⁶
 y es que quiso Dios en ella
 honrar el sexo femíneo.
 ¡Víctor, víctor!

 Ocho y diez vueltas° del sol,   turns
55 era el espacio° florido   time
 de su edad; mas de su ciencia
 ¿quién podrá contar los siglos?³⁷
 ¡Víctor, víctor!

 Perdióse ¡oh dolor! la forma
60 de sus doctos silogismos;°   arguments
 pero, los que no con tinta,

---

³⁴ This is the emperor who martyred Catherine. According to tradition, he convoked a gathering of leading intellectuals (referred to as "soberbios" in the previous line) to dispute Christianity with her. Instead, she converted many of these prominent citizens to her faith, including the emperor's wife. This provoked his wrath and subsequently her martyrdom.

³⁵ All those whom Catherine converted were martyred with her.

³⁶ **Nunca de varón...** *Never have we seen a comparable triumph from a distinguished male*

³⁷ Catherine was eighteen when she was beheaded, after being tortured on the wheel.

dejó con su sangre escritos.[38]
¡Víctor, víctor!

Tutelar° sacra patrona,   guardian
65 es de las letras° asilo;°   learning, sanctuary
    porque siempre ilustre° sabios,   may enlighten
    quien santos de sabios hizo.[39]
    ¡Víctor, víctor!

---

[38] **Pero, los que…** *But those (arguments) she left behind were written not with ink, but with (her) blood.*

[39] **Porque siempre ilustre…** *So that she who made saints out of wise men, may always enlighten wise men*

Spanish-English Glossary

A

abajo below; downward
abierto open
abismo abyss
ablandar to soften (up)
aborrecido hated
aborto freak
abrasado burning
abrazar to embrace
abrir to open
acabar to conclude; to consummate; to die; to end; to kill; —**se** to die
acaso by chance
acero steel
acertado accurate
acetar (= *aceptar*) to accept
acompañar to accompany
acongojarse to be become distressed; (*n.*) self-affliction
acrecentar to increase
acusar to accuse; to reproach
adamar to pursue
adentro inside; **más** — deeper
admirado astonished
admirarse to marvel
admitir to allow
adobado spiced
adolecer to be ill
afán desire
afectar to affect; — **paso** to move on

afición fondness; taste
afligir to hurt
afrenta insult
agonal competing
agora (= *ahora*) now
aguardiente brandy
agudo sharp; sharply
airado angry
aire air; breeze; wind;
airoso windy
ajeno alien; foreign; of someone else
alabar to praise
ala wing
albedrío free will
albergue dwelling
alborada dawn
alcanzar to manage; to obtain; to reach
alegrarse to rejoice
alejar to alienate
alemán German
algo something
algún certain; some
alguna some; — **vez** at times; on occasion
alguno someone
alimaña beast
alimento nourishment
allá elsewhere; over there; there; **más** — **de** beyond

173

alma soul
almena battlements
almo sacred
alquitara alembic
alterado agitated
alteza height
altivo arrogant
alto celestial; high; **de —** fully
alzar to raise
amada beloved lady
amado beloved; lover
amago sign
amancillado defaced
amante lover; loving
amargo bitter
amarillo pale
amarrado tied down
ámbar amber
ambulante wandering
ameno pleasant
amistad friendship
amo master
amores love; loves
amoroso loving; of love
amortecido deadened
andar to be; to walk; **andá** come on now
anegado drowned
anegarse to sink
animoso energetic
anochecer to turn to darkness; to become night
ansí (= *así*) thus
ansia anxiety; desire; longing; passion
ansioso anxious
antaños past years
antártico antarctic
antes before; previously; **— que**

before
antojos fickleness
apagar to extinguish
aparecer to appear
apartado set apart
apartar to turn away
apenas almost; barely
aplacar to calm
apolíneo Apollonian; divine
aposento room
aprendido learned
apresurarse to hasten
apretado urgent
aprieto straits
aprisionado imprisoned
apurar to examine
aquí here; **— de** come back here
arbitrio will
arca ark
arcángel archangel
arder to burn
ardiente burning; fiery
ardor warmth
arena sand
argüir to argue
armado armed; prepared
armiño ermine fur
arrabales outskirts
arrepentirse to repent; (*n.*) repentance
arriba above; upward; **boca —** face up; **de —** from heaven
arroyo stream
arte art; skill; **sin —** carelessly
artificio trick
asador roasting spit
asegurar to assure
asentado seated
asentar to settle

asido seized
asiento seat
asilo sanctuary
asistir to be present
asno donkey; nitwit
asomar to let oneself be seen; —se
(a) to go (before)
asombro amazement
aspereza cruelty; harshness
áspero harsh; rough; untamed
áspid snake
aspirar to breathe; (*n.*) breathing
atado bound; tied (up)
atenido (a) attendant (on)
atesorar to hoard
atrevido daring
atrevimiento daring
aumentar to increase
aun even; yet
aunque although; even if; even
though; though
aurora rose-colored dawn; sunrise
austro south wind
ave bird
avenirse to come to an agreement
avergonzarse (de) to be ashamed
(by)
avisar to warn
azada hoe; shovel
azucena lily

B
báculo walking stick
bajar to descend
bajel small boat
bajeza lowliness
bajo low; low-born person; lowly
balar to bleat
balbucir to stammer

bálsamo balsam
bañar to bathe
barbado bearded
bastante enough; more than enough
bastar to be enough; to suffice
batalla battle
beldad beauty
belicoso aggressive
bellota acorn
bendecir to bless
bendito blessed
benino (= *benigno*) kindly
bien blessing; contentment; good;
goodness; good thing; well —es
well-being; **no** — ill
bienaventurado blessed
blanca a type of coin; white
blanco fair; white
blancura whiteness
blando soft; tender
blasón glory
bocado bite
bodega wine cellar
bola sphere; **de** — **en** — from end to
end
bolsa purse
bosque woods
brasero hearth
bravata boasting
breve brief; cramped; tiny
brevedad brevity
brío vigor
bruñido burnished
bruto beast
burla joke
burlar to joke; to mock
buscar to seek

C

caballería cavalry
caballero gentleman
caber to fit
cadáver corpse
cadena chain
caducar to falter
caduco failed; failing; fleeting; short-lived
caer to fall
caído fallen; **por** — because he is fallen
calidad status
callado silent
caminante wanderer
camino direction; road; route; way
campo countryside; field
can dog
cantado sung
canto song
capacidad expanse
capitán captain
cara beloved; dear; face; obverse
caracol snail
cárcel jail; prison
carga load
carillo my dear one
carmesí crimson
carne flesh
carrera race
carro chariot
caso case; incident
castaña chestnut
castigar to punish
casual chance occurrence
catedrático professor
cativo (= *cautivo*) captive
caudal wealth
cauteloso crafty

cauterio cautery
cautivo captive
cavar to dig
caverna cavern; depth
cazador hunter
cebada barley
cedro cedar
celada hiding; **en** — concealed
celestial heavenly
celo envy, jealousy
ceniza ash
censura condemnation
centella spark
centro center; deep sea
ceño frown
cercado surrounded
cercar to surround
cerco circle; siege; wall
cerrado enclosed
cerrar to close; to enclose
cesar to cease; to end; to stop
cetro scepter
chopo poplar
ciego blind
cielo heaven; sky; **—s** heaven; heavens
ciencia knowledge
cierto certain; sure; surely
ciervo stag; deer
cierzo north wind
cítara cithara, zither
clamar to cry out
claro bright; clear
clavado nailed
clavel carnation
cobrar to recover, regain
coco bogeyman
codicia envy
codicioso eager

coger to catch; to gather; to kiss; to pick
collado hill
colocado positioned
colorido colorful
coluna (= *columna*) column
combate skirmish
combatir to break down
comer to eat
cometa comet; warning sign
comigo (= *conmigo*) with me
comodidad comfort
compaña companion
compasarse (con) to pace oneself (with)
competir to compete
compuesto (de) composed (of)
concebir to conceive
concha shell
concorde concordant, harmonious
condenado condemned
condenar to condemn
confesar to confess
confianza confidence
confusamente in confusion
congojarse (= *acongojarse*) to become distressed; (*n.*) self-affliction
conjurar to beseech
conocer to know; to recognize; **—se** to become aware of oneself
conocido recognized
consejar (= *aconsejar*) to advise
consejo advice; good advice
consentimiento consent
consentir (en) to allow
considerar to consider; to see
consonante harmonious; rhyme
consumir to consume; **—se** to destroy oneself

contar to count; to tell (about)
contentamiento contentment
contento content; happiness;
contino (= *continuo*) continuously; **de —** always; for all eternity
conveniencia suitable thing
convertido attuned; transformed
convertirse to change, transform
corazón heart
cordura good judgment; sanity
coro chorus
coronado crowned
coronar to achieve
corredor scout
corregir to control
correr to run; to run toward; to spread
corriente current; flowing; stream
cortar to cut; to fly through
corvo bent
cosa anything; thing
costilla rib
costumbre custom
crecer to grow
criada maid
criado raised; **mal —** ill-mannered
criador creator
criar to produce
cristal body of water; crystal; glass
cristalino clear
criaturas all of nature; creature
crucificado crucified
cruel cruel; **por —** for being cruel
cualquier any; **a — hora** at any time
cualquiera anyone; either one
cuán how
cuanto all that; as; how much; **todos —s** all who
cuánto how; how much; (*pl.*) how

many
cuarteto quatrain
cuarto quarter (coin)
cubierto covered; roofed
cubrir to cover
cuchillo knife
cuello neck
cuero leather
cuidado care; cares; concern;
  suffering; worries
cuidar to care (for)
cuitado aggrieved (person)
culebra snake
culpa blame; fault
culpar to blame; to criticize
cultura cultivation
cumbre mountain top, summit
cuna cradle
curar to care; to heal
cuyo whose

D
dama beloved woman; lady
daño damage; harm
dar to give
deber to be fitting; to ought to; to
  owe
débil weak
decir to say; to tell
decoro chastity
dejar to leave (behind); — **de** (+
  infinitive) to stop (an action);
  —**se** to leave oneself; to let oneself
delante previous
deleite delight
deleitoso delightful
delgado skinny
delito crime
demás others; **lo(s)** — everything

else
denfadado (= *desenfadado*) soothed
denuedo bravery
depingir to paint
derecho proper; rights
derramar to pour (out)
desalentado discouraged
desatado melted
desatar to release; —**se** to flow
desatino folly
descaminado lost
descansado restful
descansar to rest
descender to descend
desconocer to disregard; to lose
descortesía impoliteness
descubrir to discover; to find
desde from
desdén disdain
desdeñar to disdain
desdeñoso disdainful
desdichado miserable
deseado desired
desear to desire
desengaño disillusion
desenlazar to liberate, unchain
deshacer to destroy
deshecho undone
desierto desert
desigual unequal
desmandado disobedient
desmayado fainting
desmayo fainting, swoon
desmentir to deny
desmoronado crumbling
desnudo stripped
desordenar to disorder
despedir to release
despeñado headlong

despertar to awaken
despierto watchful
despojos rubble
desposado betrothed
despreciar to scorn
después after; — **que** after; since
desterrado exiled
desterrar to exile
destierro exile
destinado destined
destinar to destine; to make
destrozo destruction
desvarío absurdity
desvelos restlessness
desventura misery; misfortune;
  unhappiness
detenerse to hold still; to linger; to
  take time
determinarse to be determined
deuda debt
dibujado sketched
dibujar to design
dichoso blissful; happy
diestro skilled; skillful
difunto dead man
dilatarse to span
diligencia effort
dinero money
discurrir to flow, to run
disfrazado disguised
distinto clear
divino divine; **bien** — divine good
do donde
doblón doubloon (coin)
docto expert; learned
dolencia pain
doliente sorrowful
dolor pain; sorrow
domesticado conquered

dominio command; domination;
  rule
don sir
doña lady; miss
donaire charm
dorado gilded, golden
dudar to doubt
dudoso doubtful
duelo affliction; trouble
dulzura sweetness
durar to endure; to last; to remain
dureza hardness
duro tough; hard

E
eclipsado extinguished
edad age; epoch; time; youth; —
  dorada golden youth
edificado built
efeto (= *efecto*) effect
ejido pasture
elogio praise
embebecido occupied
emisión outpouring
empañar to mist up
empedernido hardened
en in; into
enamorado in love
enamorar to endear; to inspire love;
  —**se (de)** to fall in love (with)
encarado featured; **mal** — ugly-
  looking
encaramar to praise
encarnar to incarnate
encender to inflame
encerrado imprisoned
encerrar to enclose; to lock
encogido shrinking
encuentro encounter

enclavarse (en) to become focussed (on)
enero January; winter
enfadar to anger
enfado anger
engañado deceived
engañador deceptive
engañar to deceive
engaño deceit, deception
engañoso deceitful
engendrado born; conceived
enherbolado herbed; poisoned with herbs
enhiesto upright
enlazado joined
enojo trouble
enojoso bothersome
ensalzar to exalt
enseñanza example
enseñar to show; to teach
entender to hear; to understand
entendido understood; **lo —** the rational mind
entendimiento understanding; rational mind
enternecer to tame
entero entirely
enterrado buried
enterrar to bury
entrañas bowels; feelings; innards; innermost recesses;
entregado given over
entregar to hand over; **—se** to give in; to surrender oneself
entretejido interwoven
entretener to entertain; to play with
enturbiar to trouble
enviar to send
envidia envy

envidiado envied
envidioso envious
érase (from *ser*) there once was
errado failed; sinful
errar to stray; to wander
error erring; error; wanderings
escala ladder
escama scale
escarmiento cautionary example
escarnecido mocked
esclarecido illustrious
escoger to assemble, compose; to choose, select
escogido chosen; picked
esconder to hide
escondido hidden; shrouded; **a —s de** hidden from
escrevir (= *escribir*) to write
escriba scribe
escrito writing; written
escudero squire
escudo shield; a type of coin; **— de armas** coat of arms
escuridad (= *oscuridad*) darkness
escuro (= *oscuro*) dark
esfera sphere
esmaltado adorned
esmeralda emerald
espacio space; time; while; **de —** for a while
espada sword; **peje —** swordfish
espantar to disturb; to scare; **—se** to be amazed; to get scared
esparcido scattered
esparcir to scatter, spread out
espejo mirror
esperanza hope
espesura thicket; thickness
espía spy

espolón heavy spur
esposo spouse
espuela spur
esquivo distant; unfriendly
estado condition; state; status
estar to be; — en sí to be alright; to be rational
estío summer
estraño (= *extraño*) strange
estrecho close; cramped; intimate
estrellado starry
etéreo heavenly
eterno eternal
excepción privilege
excusar to exempt
expósito abandoned
extranjero foreign; outside
extraño strange
extremado beautiful

F
fabricado built; created
fácil easy; por — for being easy
faltar to be absent, missing; to lack
favor favor; kindness
fe faith
femíneo feminine
fiar to entrust
fiera brute; wild beast
fiero beastly; fierce; ugly; wild
figura bodily form; face
figurarse to imagine
filomena nightingale
fin end
fingido false
finito finite, limited
firme stable
flecha arrow
florecer to bloom

florecido blooming
florido flowery; of flowers
fontana fount, spring
forastero foreigner
forzado constrained
francés French
freno bit; brake
frente forehead
fresco cool
frontera frontier
fuente fount, spring
fuera out; outside; — de away from
fuero law
fuerte strong; strong man
fuerza power; strength
fugitivo fleeting
fundar to base an opinion
funesto mournful
furia fury; rage

G
gala finery; jewel
galán gallant
galera warship
gallardía intensity
gallardo brave
gamo buck
ganadero cattle rancher
ganado herd (of cattle); won
ganar to win (over); —se to gain oneself
gastado spent
gato moneybag; thief
gemido moan; con — moaning
gemir to moan
gentil elegant; gentle; graceful
gentileza gentility
gesto face
girar to thrash

gobernado directed
gobernar to govern
gobierno government
godo Goth
golfo gulf
gozar to enjoy; enjoyment
gracia grace; **—s** graces; thanks
gracioso graceful
granada pomegranate
granado upstanding
grande big; grandee; great
grandeza grandeur, greatness
grave grave; grievous
gravedad seriousness
griego Greek
grito shout
guardar to guard; to look after; to
    respect **—se (de)** to guard
    (oneself) against; to keep distance
    (from)
guerrero warrior
guía guide
guiar to guide
guirnalda garland
gustar to please; to taste; **— de** to
    enjoy
gusto pleasure; whim

H
haber to have (aux.); **—** de to be
    expected to; to be obliged to; to be
    scheduled to
habitación dwelling
habitar to dwell
hábito clothing; custom
hacia towards
hado fate
hallado found
hallar to find

harto sufficient
haz face
hebra thread
hecho done; fact; made; **de —** indeed
helado icy
herido wounded
herir to wound
hermosura beauty
hielo ice
hierro shackle
hilo thread
holgar (de) to be pleased (to)
hombro shoulder
homicida murderous
honesto chaste
honrado honorably
honrar to honor
hora hour; time; **a cualquier —** at
    any time; **en — buena** as much as
    you like; best wishes
hospedado lodged
hospedaje hospitality
hospedar to host
hoy today; **de —** from today
    onwards
huella footprint
huerto garden; orchard
hueso bone
huésped guest; traveler
huida flow
huir to flee (from)
humilde humble
humillarse to humble oneself
humo smoke
humor blood; mood
hurtar to steal

I
ido gone

ignorante ignorant; unknowledgeable

ignorar to ignore; to not heed

igual equal; **sin —** unequaled

igualar to make the same size

ilustrar to enlighten

ilustre distinguished; highly esteemed

imperio empire

importunar to bother

importuno annoying; pressing

imprimir to impart

incierto unsure

incitar to provoke

inconsecuente illogical

Indias Indies

infamar to slander

infierno hell

ingratamente thanklessly

ingratitud ingratitude

ingrato ungrateful

inmensidad immensity

inmenso immense; **lo —** the immenseness

inmortal eternal; immortal

innumerable countless

inscribir to write

instancia entreaty

ínsula isle

interés benefit

ira anger

ir to go; to pass by; **— se** to leave; to slip away

J

jamás ever; never

jaspe jasper

jornada expedition

jornal day's wage; **a —** paid by the day

juez judge

juntamente together

juntar to assemble; to bring together; to unite **— se** to unite

junto together

justiciero fair

justo just, fair

juzgar to judge

L

laberinto labyrinth

labio lip

labrar to embroider

ladera hillside

lado side

lagar winepress

lama mud silt

lamentable mournful

lamentarse to lament

lástima pity

latir yelping

lazo noose

lecho bed

lengua language; speech; tongue

letras learning

letrero sign

levante east wind

leve light

liberal generous

librado delivered, rescued

libre free

lidiar to fight

ligero fleeting; gentle; swift; swiftly

lilio lily

limado worn away

limar to erode

limbo border

lira lyre

lisonja flattery
lisonjero flattering; pleasing
liviandad moral looseness
liviano unchaste
llaga wound
llagar to wound
llama flame
llamar to call (on); (*n.*) knocking
llano meadow; plain
llanto weeping
llegar to arrive; to come
lleno filled
llevar to plunge; to take (away)
llorar to cry; to lament; to mourn; to weep
lloro weeping
llover to rain down
locura madness
logro profit; **a —** for a profit
loor praise
lozano vigorous
luciente shining
lugar place; **en — de** instead of
lumbre light
luz light

M
madona ma'am
maestro teacher; master; **el gran —** God
magisterio lesson
majada sheepfold
majestad dignity; majesty
mal bad ending; bad situation; evil; ill; illness; misfortune; suffering
maltratar to mistreat
malvado wicked
manar to flow
mancha spot

manera manner; way; **de tal —** in such a way
manso gentle; meek
mantequilla butter
manzano apple tree
mañana morning; tomorrow
maravillado amazed
maravillar to amaze
marchitar to destroy
mármol marble
mas but
más furthermore; more; most; the most
materia material
mayor greater; greatest
mayordomo steward
medalla medal
medianoche midnight
medida measure; size
medio half; middle
medir to measure
medula marrow
mejilla cheek
mejorado better; in a better way
mejorar to better; to improve; **—se** to get better
menear to sway
menos less; shorter; **lo —** the lowest
menoscabar to diminish
menosprecio contempt
mensajero messenger
mentido deceptive
menudo fine
mercader merchant
merced mercy
merecer to be worthy
mesilla little table
meta goal
metafísico philosophical

metido immersed; placed
mezclado mixed
miedo fear; **tener —** to be afraid; to fear
mientras while
milagro miracle
minero mine (containing metals or jewels); origins
mirado viewed
mirar to look, gaze; to consider; (*n.*) gaze; **—se** to be seen; to see oneself
mismo same
mitad half
modo kind, type; **de ese —** in that way; **de varios —s** in various ways
molesto troublesome
monarquía kingdom, monarchy
moneda coin
monstruo monster
monte woodland
montiña (= *montaña*) mountain
monumento tomb
morada dwelling
morar to dwell; to stay
morcilla blood sausage
morder to bite; to gnaw; to nip
moreno dark
morir to die; (*n.*) death; **—se** to die; to wither
moro Moor; Muslim
mortaja funeral shroud
mortal deadly; mortal man
mosto juice
mostrar to show
mover to move; **—se** to move about
mozo young man
muchedumbre multitude

mudanza change
mudar to change; **—se** to change
mudo mute
muerto dead; killed; killing
mundanal worldly
muralla wall
muro (outside) wall
musa muse; inspiration
músico musician
mustio withered

N

nacer to be born
nacido born
nada nothing; nothingness
naranjada orangeade
naufragio shipwreck
navegar to navigate
navío ship
necedad foolishness
necio foolish; stupid; useless
negación self-denial
negar to deny; **—se** to deny oneself; to refuse
nemoroso wooded
nevado snowy
nido nest
nieve snow; **de —** with snow
ninfa nymph
ninguno nobody
nivel level; **con desigual —** inconsistently
nocturnar to spend the night
notado mentioned; noticed; observed
nublado cloud

O

obedecer to obey; (*n.*) obedience

obligar to oblige
obrar to work; — **bien** to be good; to do good works
obras deeds; works
obscurecerse (= *oscurecerse*) to darken
obscuro dark
obstentar (= *ostentar*) to show (off)
ocasión cause
ocaso sunset
ocupar to employ
odio hatred
oficio occupation
oído ear
oír to hear
olor fragrance
olvidado forgetting; forgotten; oblivious
olvidarse to not think of oneself
olvido forgetfulness; oblivion
onda wave
opinión reputation
orear to blow
oriente sunrise; the East
orilla riverbank
oro gold; **como un** — neat as a pin
os you
oscuro dark; **a oscuras** in darkness
ostentar to brag; to display; to show
otero knoll
otro another; any other; other; other person; **o** —**s** other; others; other people
ovas algae
oveja sheep

P

pacer to graze
padecer to suffer; (*n.*) suffering

Padre God
paga pay
paja straw
palestra arena; fray; place
palomica little dove
pañal diaper
par equal; **en** — **de** at the same time as
para against; in order to; — **que** in order that, so that
parar to pause; to stop
parecer to appear; to seem; (*n.*) way of thinking; — **a** to resemble
Parnaso Parnassus; circle of poets
parte part; place; side; **a todas** —**s** all around **de mi** — in my favor
partir to leave; **al** — upon leaving
parto birth; offspring
pasajero traveler
pasado passed; past; **de** — in passing
pasar to pass; to remain; —**se** to pass away
pasión intense suffering; passion
paso progress; route; step
pastel pastry
pasto pasture
pastor shepherd
pastoral rustic
patraña old story
patria homeland; nation
patrona (fem. of *patrón*) patron saint
pecar to sin
pecho breast; chest; heart
pedazo piece
pegado stuck
peligro danger; risk
peligroso dangerous
pena grief; pain; sorrow

penar to suffer
pensamiento thought
pensar to think
perder to lose; to destroy
perdidizo lost
perdido lost; misguided
perecedero dying
perecer to die
peregrino foreign; pilgrim; wanderer
perfeto (= *perfecto*) perfect
perfumear to perfume
permanecer to remain
perseverar to persevere
pesado heavy
pez fish
pie foot; footing; poetic meter
piedad comfort; compassion; grace; hospitality; pity
piel fur
píldora pill
pincel artist's brush
piña cluster
pisar to tread
placer joy
planta foot
plata silver; **de —** silvery
plateado silvery
pluma feather; **de —** feathery
pobre modest; poor man
poder power; to be able; to have power, to manage to
poderoso powerful
poetisa female poet
polvo dust
polvoroso dusty
pompa splendor
ponzoñoso poisonous
por for; for being; in order to; through; **— donde** whereby; **— ti** because of you; for your own defense
porción portion
pordiosero beggar
porfía competition
porfiar to insist on; to persist
porque because; so that, in order that
pos after; **en — de** behind
posada lodging
posesión possession; **en la —** once possessed
posta hitching post
postrera (*fem. of* postrer) final
prado meadow
precepto commandment
preciar to value
precipitado hurled
pregonera proclaiming
prenda control; pledge; token of commitment
preso imprisoned; prisoner
prestar to lend
presto quick; soon
presumido conceited
presumir to presume
presunción presumption
presupuesto presupposed; **por —** as a given
presura haste
presuroso hastily; swift
pretender to seek; to try
pretendida pursued; **para —** in pursuit
primavera spring, springtime; youth
primores beauty; delight
principal great; illustrious person; noble; wealthy
príncipe prince

probar to experience; to test
procurar to seek; to try
prodigio marvel
producido born
profano worldly
prometido promised
propio intrinsic
proporción proportion
proprio (= *propio*) own
proseguir to follow
provecho advantage; **sin —** for naught
prueba proof
pudo (3rd person singular preterit of *poder*)
puente bridge
puerto haven
pues because; since; well; **— que** since
puesto made; placed
punición punishment
punto dot; moment; point
puro pure; clear
púrpura purple
purpúreo purple

Q

quebrado broken
quebrantar to break
quebrar to break; **—se** to crash
quedar to become; to continue; to end up; to remain **—se** to remain
quejarse to complain
quejoso complaining
querella complaint
querer to love; to want; to strive; to try; to seek
querido lover
quien who; whom; whoever; he who; she who; someone who; someone; the person who; anyone
quiso (3rd person singular preterit of *querer*)
quitar to remove; to take away
quito freed

R

rabiar to go mad
ramillete cluster of flowers
ramo branch
raposa fox
raro strange
rato short time; while
razón grounds; reason; reasoning ability
razonar to reason
razones words
real royal; a type of coin
recatarse to act prudently
recato modesty
recelar to suspect
recelo suspicion
reclinado lying
reclinar to lean
recordar to recall, remember; to awaken
recrear to delight
recuerdo reminder
redención redemption
redimir to redeem
referir to reveal; to tell
refrenar to restrain
regalado caressing
regalar caress
regar to water
regido governed
regidor councilman
regir to control; to rule

reinar to reign, rule
reírse (de) to laugh (about)
relámpago lightning bolt
relevado chiseled
reloj clock; — **de sol** sundial
reluciente shining (bright)
relumbrar to shine
remedio remedy
remo oar
rendido surrendered
renovar to renew
reparado restored
repartir to share
repente suddenness; **de** — suddenly;
    urgent
reportado calm
reposar to rest
reposo tranquility, rest, repose
repuesto hidden
repugnar to detest
resguardo safeguard
respirar to breathe
resplandecer to shine
resplandeciente shining
resplandores radiance, shining;
    splendor
respuesta answer
restar to remain
restituido brought back
restituir to give back
retirarse to withdraw
retrato portrait
reventar to sizzle
reverenciar to respect deeply
revolver to wield
ribera riverside; shore
riesgo risk
rigor severity
roble oak tree

robo stolen item
rocín meager
rocío dew
rodeado surrounded
rodearse to revolve
rodela round-shaped shield
roer to gnaw
rogado begged; beseeched; **de** —
    because she is begged
rogar to beg; to woo
rompido broken
rondar to threaten to return
rosado pink; rosy
rosal rose bush
rostro face
roto broken; wrecked
rubio blond; golden
rueda wheel
ruego request
ruido noise; noisy quarrels; sound
ruiseñor nightingale

S
saber to know; (*n.*) knowledge; — **a**
    to taste of
sabio wise (man)
sabor flavor; taste **a su** — in delight
sabroso delicious; delightful
sacar to remove
sacro holy; sacred
saeta arrow
sagaz shrewd; wise
sagrado holy, sacred
sala chamber
salida death; exit
salir to emerge; to go; to leave; —**se**
    a to go out into
salmo psalm
saltador leaping

salteado attacked
saltear to assault
sanar to heal
saña fury
sangre blood
sanguinoso bloody
santo saint
sayón executioner
secar to dry
secreto secretly
sed thirst
seguido followed
seguir to pursue; —**se** to redound
según according to; given how
seguro safe; sure
sello seal
semblantes countenance
sembrar to sow
semejante fellow
sencillo coin of low value
senda path
seno breast; refuge
sentido feeling; sense; senses
sentir to detect; to feel; to perceive; to regret
seña gesture
señal target
señalado famous; pointed out
Señor Lord
sepultado buried; wrapped
sepultura tomb
ser to be; (*n*.) being
serena (= *sirena*) siren
serenarse to become calm
sereno calm
servicio of service
servir (de) serve (as)
seso mind
severo harsh; severe; strict

sí herself; himself; itself; themselves
sierpe serpent; snake
siglo century
significar to indicate
signo sign
silbo whistling
silogismo argument; syllogism
sino but also; but rather; except
siquiera if you please
soberano sovereign; supreme
soberbio proud; spirited
sobre atop; up on
sobresalir to stand out
socio mate
sois (2ⁿᵈ person plural present indicative of *ser*)
soledad solitude
soler to be in the habit (of)
solicitar to seek; to woo
solo alone; **a solas** alone
sólo only; **no —** not only
sombra shadow
sometido subdued
son melody; sound
sonante sounding
sonar to sound
sonoro sounding
sonoroso sounding
soñar to dream; (*n*.) dreaming
soñoliento drowsy
sortija ring
sosegado calm, quiet, tranquil
sosegar to end
sospechar to suspect
sostenido supported
soto grove
suave gentle; kind; soft
subido high
sublime lofty

suceder to supplant
sudor sweat
suelo earth, ground; Earth
sueño dream; rest; sleep
suerte fate; luck; **de la** — in the
    manner; **de tal** — in such a way
sufrir to suffer
sujeto under control
sumido submerged
sumo greatest; supreme
superlativo exaggerated
suspirar to sigh
sustentado supported
sutileza subtlety

T
tal in such a way; such
tálamo wedding bed
tamaño size
tan as; so; so much; such
tanto so much; such; **—s** so many; **en**
    — que as long as; while
tardar to be late; to delay
tasa price; rate; **sin** — without limit
techo ceiling
tejer to weave
tela cloth; veil
temer to fear
temeroso fearful
temido feared
temor fear
tempestad storm
tempestuoso stormy
templado tempered
temprano early-blooming
tendido hung; stretched out
tenebroso shadowy
tener to have
teñido stained

terceto tercet
terneza tenderness
tesoro treasure
testigo witness
tiempo time; **a su** — in turn; **mis —s**
    my days
tiernamente tenderly
tierno soft
tierra earth; grave; land
tino aim; good sense
tinta ink
tirano tyrannical
tirar to shoot
tocar to touch; — **a uno** to fall to
    someone (to do something, etc.)
todo all; each; — **cuanto** all that; **—s**
    everybody
toque touch
torcer to twist
tormento torment
tornarse to become; to return
torpe crude
tortolica little turtledove
traer to bear; to bring; to carry; to
    keep; to wear
traje attire
tras after; behind
trasformado (= *transformado*)
    changed
traspasar to pass through
trasunto representation
tratar to deal; to treat
trato dealing
tristura sadness
triunfar to triumph
triunfo triumph
trocar to change
troncado crushed
trovador troubadour

turar (= *durar*) to stay
turbar to upset
tutelar guardian

U
último final; ultimate
ultrajar to insult
umbral threshold

V
vagar to wander freely
vajilla tableware
valentía bravery
valer to be worth
valiente brave
valor value; worth
vano vain; **en —** in vain; **vanamente** pointlessly
varón male; man
vega meadow
vejez old age
velador wakeful
velocidad speed
veloz swiftly
vena flood; mineral vein; stream; vein
vencer to conquer; to triumph (over)
vencido conquered
vengado avenged
venida arrival
venir to come
ventar fanning
ventura chance; happiness; **por —** by chance
verbo word; **el Verbo** the Word
verdadero true
verdura green; greenness
verse to see oneself

verso poetry; verse
vestido clothed
vestir to attire, dress; **—se (de)** to clothe oneself (in)
vez time; turn; **alguna —** on occasion
víctor (= *vítor*) hurray
vidro (= *vidrio*) glass
viento wind; **al —** in the wind
vil despicable
viña vineyard
viola violet
violado raped
vista sight; **a — de** at the sight of
vivido lived; **lo —** the past
vivir to live; (*n.*) life
vivo alive; intense; lively; living; **medio —** half-alive
voces shouts
volador flying
volar to fly; to flutter
volcán volcano
voluntad will
volverse to become; to return
vos you
vuelo flight; flutter
vuelta rotation; turn; **dar —s** to revolve
vuelto changed, transformed
vuestro your
vulgo common people
vulnerado wounded

Y
ya ever; now; still; yet; **— que** since
yacer to lie, recline

Z
zaga rear; **a — de** following

CPSIA information can be obtained
at www.ICGtesting.com
Printed in the USA
BVHW070612180119
538145BV00004B/50/P

9 781589 770485